SELF-ESTEEM
GOD'S WAY

IDENTIFY WHAT THE WORLD TELLS US
AND DISCOVER GOD'S VIEW

KATHY SEBO, LCSW

WESTBOW
PRESS®
A DIVISION OF THOMAS NELSON
& ZONDERVAN

WestBow Press books may be ordered through booksellers or by contacting:

WestBow Press
A Division of Thomas Nelson & Zondervan
1663 Liberty Drive
Bloomington, IN 47403
www.westbowpress.com
1 (866) 928-1240

Scriptures taken from the Holy Bible, New International Version®, NIV®. Copyright © 1973, 1978, 1984, 2011 by Biblica, Inc.™ Used by permission of Zondervan. All rights reserved worldwide. www.zondervan.com The "NIV" and "New International Version" are trademarks registered in the United States Patent and Trademark Office by Biblica, Inc.™

ISBN: 978-1-9736-9727-5 (sc)
ISBN: 978-1-9736-9729-9 (hc)
ISBN: 978-1-9736-9728-2 (e)

Library of Congress Control Number: 2020913178

Print information available on the last page.

WestBow Press rev. date: 08/10/2020

CONTENTS

PART 3: WHAT HEALTHY SELF-ESTEEM LOOKS LIKE

INTRODUCTION

I embarked on writing this book because of my work in counseling. I am in a private practice working with kids, adults, marriages, families, and groups. This book is an accumulation and a compilation of the experiences in my years of working in this field. I viewed clients' misperception of self-esteem and realized that they were focusing on many of the wrong things. These kept them from feeling how they should about themselves. I want you to start this book with an open mind and let God tell you clearly what your focus should be.

Self-esteem is all about how much we feel loved, valued, accepted, and thought well of by others or by God. Our self-esteem is important because how we feel about ourselves influences how we live our lives. There are many clues from the Bible that help us to know what we should feel about ourselves according to how God feels about us.

> For you created my inmost being; you knit me together in my mother's womb. I praise you because I am fearfully and wonderfully made; your works are wonderful; I know that full well. My frame was not hidden from you when I was made in the secret place. When I was woven together in the depths of the earth, your eyes saw my unformed body. All the days ordained for me were written in your book before one of them came to be. (Psalm 139:13–16)

He created us just the way He wanted us. Each of us is an original.

The world declares war on our souls and sets unreachable standards that define who we are and how we should feel about ourselves. The world looks at the outward appearance. God has a different standard. "But the

Lord said to Samuel, 'Do not consider his appearance or his height, for I have rejected him. The Lord does not look at the things man looks at. *Man looks at the outward appearance, but the Lord looks at the heart.*'" (1 Samuel 16:7; italics mine).

We will explore the things that are a part of the world's definition of who we are and how that affects our self-esteem. We will also look at the spiritual mindset of how to have an accurate assessment of how we should feel about ourselves. The world's mindset of self-esteem is contrary to God's vision for us. He has given us His glorious Word so that we can find the best way to live. Surely, the God who created us is able to tell us who we are. So I invite you to open your mind to a different way of developing your self-esteem. It is less about how you feel about yourself and more about how God feels about you.

Satan has gone to war against us. He wants us to believe all the lies the world tells us about ourselves. He wants us to believe everything that is contrary to God. However, God is fighting the battle for us. Everything that God wants us to believe will be contrary to what the world tells us. We must take hold of the biblical concepts that God has given us.

> Therefore, I urge you, brothers, in view of God's mercy, to offer your bodies as living sacrifices, holy and pleasing to God—this is your spiritual act of worship. *Do not conform any longer to the pattern of this world, but be transformed by the renewing of your mind.* Then you will be able to test and approve what God's will is, His good and perfect will. (Romans 12:1–2; italics mine)

Our bodies are not our own. We need to offer them to God. This is how we worship God and please Him. We cannot accept the standard the world uses to define who we are. God asks us to transform our minds—to think differently. Once we do this change of thinking, then we can determine what God's will is for our lives. Welcome to the journey into a changed way of thinking.

WORLD'S INFLUENCE

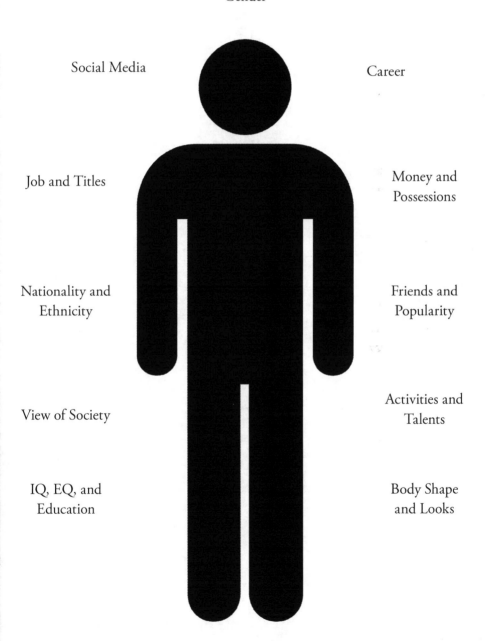

Gender

Social Media

Career

Job and Titles

Money and
Possessions

Nationality and
Ethnicity

Friends and
Popularity

View of Society

Activities and
Talents

IQ, EQ, and
Education

Body Shape
and Looks

PART 1

THE WORLD'S DEFINITION OF SELF-ESTEEM

We are inundated with messages in the world from magazines, models, movies, newspapers, advertising, the internet, Facebook, and many more. Those who have low self-esteem struggle with insecurity, jealousy, anger, fear, selfishness, and guilt. The world tells us how we should look, feel, achieve, and present ourselves in a manner that makes others have positive thoughts toward us. This would require us to control others' feelings toward us at home, work, school, church, and social events. Wow. I'm exhausted already just thinking about how much energy that would take! "We long for approval, yet when conditions placed upon that approval, we believe we are worth wherever we land on the measuring stick of the standards set for us" *(Beautiful Lies,* by Jennifer Strickland). Parents, teachers, and other authority figures influence the ideas we develop about ourselves. In childhood, if these individuals spent more time criticizing than praising, it can be detrimental to our self-esteem. Many have heard negative messages from their past, such as "You're not smart enough to make it to college." "Get your head out of the clouds. Stop dreaming." "You're rotten. I wish I'd never had you." "You're stupid." "Be quiet. Nobody cares what you think." These statements have actually been said to clients of mine as children. Satan loves these messages. Satan loves any message that tears us down and draws us to his lies. He tempts adults to accept the things that they were told as kids to be true. They still hear in their heads the negative messages and often repeat them to themselves as self-talk. They begin to believe these messages as representations of who they really are. One would think that since they didn't like hearing those messages as kids they wouldn't continue to perpetuate the messages as adults. But what we find is that they're tapes that become so ingrained in our brains that they're difficult to break. How could anyone have positive thoughts toward himself or herself with such negative messages?

It can be difficult to achieve the world's standard of what is praiseworthy. Many of the categories that the world upholds as praiseworthy are things that we don't even want for ourselves or consider important. Take, for example, "people pleasers" who want everyone to like them and would do everything to achieve that. If your goal is to have everyone like you, then you become what you think others want you to be. In essence, you become a chameleon who changes colors depending upon what group you are surrounded by. The problem with morphing is that you become unsure of who you really are and what you really think and feel about life.

Another group who are trapped are the "conflict avoiders" who are not willing to stand up for what they really think and are pulled by those they are around. When there is a conflict between God's truth and the world's truths, some avoid conflict and will not speak up for what's right and true. When that person doesn't want to speak up, there is a lack of resolve that can cause unwanted stress and distance in relationships. Many are also swayed by peer pressure. There's a saying from a catalog that states,

> I choose to live by choice, not by chance. To make changes, not excuses. To be motivated, not manipulated. To be useful, not used. To excel, not compete. I choose self-esteem, not self-pity. I choose to listen to my inner voice, not the random opinion of others (no author noted).

"We are influenced by our peer group and those we choose to hang out with. Do not be misled: Bad company corrupts good character," says 1 Corinthians 15:33.

How have others' opinions affected your self-image?

Do you fall into any of these categories?

Which ones do you relate to?

The definition of *identity* asks the questions "Who am I?" and "What defines me and my character?" Identity provides a sense of one's self and one's individuality. We are going to divide and discuss individually the specific ways the world defines *self-esteem*. This will not be an all-inclusive list, so add to the list as you think of other ways that the world defines how they see you and how you see yourself.

ONE

GENDER

Gender is a variable that can affect self-esteem. Some cultures place more importance on male children. There are cultures that even try to discard the female children because they want to have a male child to bring the family honor. Different roles are placed on men and women. We have no control on what gender we are, unless we choose to change it medically. The culture and ethnicity often influence the importance placed on gender. Our gender affects how we feel about ourselves. Males are typically thought to have quicker-rebounding egos, self-images, and self-esteem than females do. Historically males have not been as actively concerned with their physical appearance as females. Men have more pressure to provide financially for their families and often for their extended families as well. If they are not providing for their families in a way that they expect of themselves, or that their family expects of them, then it can contribute to a lower self-esteem. There are times when the husband's wife makes more money than he does, which can affect his self-esteem. Women are more reactive to the evaluations of others and more relationally focused than men. Men are more focused on action and achievement. Women in the working world often receive lower salaries than men in the same job position. There is a continual pressure on females to strive to become a "model image." Women have a lot of pressure on them to be great mothers, wives, homemakers, and employees. If women don't perform all these roles well, their self-esteem suffers. Women are expected to multitask and find balance in all their roles. When they cannot perform in every area, chances are that their expectations may be too high.

Most may already be aware that there are physical differences between men and women. We have all heard the saying, "Men are from Mars and women are from Venus." Many are probably aware that women are better at multitasking and men are better at performing one task at a time. Women are normally more social and use more words in a day than men. Women are therefore better at social thinking and interactions. Women have more connections between the right and left sides of their brains, which allows them to think and feel at the same time. Men, on the other hand, have fewer connections and are more apt to think than feel. This is why we say that men need to hide in their "man caves" to figure out what they feel. It takes time for them to figure out what they feel because they do not have as many connections in their brains on the emotional side. Because of this difference, it may make it more difficult to deal with others' emotions. Men like to solve problems when feelings are shared with them, and women are more likely to just listen. Men are generally better with coordination and controlling their movements and have faster reaction times. Women, though, generally have better memory capacity than men. If you have ever wondered why women seem like collectors of situations from the past, it is a biological difference. Men tend to have a better spatial and geographic memory and sense of direction. As a funny example, women definitely stop more often to ask for directions than men.

Seeing is another difference in men and women. The male's retina is actually thicker than a female's. This allows men to track larger objects and women to see more texture and color. Women hear better, whereas men are able to drown out unwanted sounds. Have you ever noticed that women go to the bathroom together in pairs and men go to the bathroom alone? Women like to do things in groups and enjoy shared experiences. Women exhibit a stronger emotional response to the anticipation of pain and are more easily startled. Men are more likely to take risks and to overestimate their abilities. Aggression or anger is expressed differently as well. For example, teen guys will get in a fist fight and girls will use their words to hurt each other. Men and women have different types of friendships.

Women have friends to help as emotional support. Men's friendships revolve around common interests, activities, competition, and work.

The world definitely places different expectations on men and women. There are obviously many differences between the two biologically as well as how society treats each gender. Both genders have a strong desire to be viewed positively and be praised by others. Since we were all created differently, our views of our gender affect the value placed on our self-worth.

How do you feel about your gender?

Have you ever wished that you were the other gender?

What type of pressure does society place on your gender?

How does that influence how you feel about yourself?

TWO

SOCIAL MEDIA

The use of social media can influence our self-esteem. Our social media profiles are an extension of our identities, according to Ray Williams in an article from *Psychology Today.* "It makes our posts, pictures and activities feel like virtual possessions or pieces of ourselves" (Bustle, Newsome, "7 Ways Social Media Can Affect Your Self-Esteem" (2016). This could make us prey for marketers who want to help us make perfect photos to increase our popularity, viewers, and how many likes we receive. This keeps us in a place where we equate self-worth with stuff, which can be our social media profiles. The more we compare ourselves to others on social media sites, such as Facebook, Snapchat, LinkedIn, Pinterest, Instagram, and YouTube, the more depressed we can get. We forget to take into account that a lot of what we are seeing is carefully orchestrated hype and not reality. Social media can lead us to assume that everyone else is feeling and living better than we are. This isn't a representation of a person's whole life. It's not even a reflection of reality but merely a glimpse of the life a person chooses to present. Posts by friends and family tend to be the best versions of themselves and their lives. We see smiling selfies with perfectly applied makeup, nice outfits, and fun places, and we forget that there are plenty of times where pictures were not flattering and times when they were not having fun.

The reality is that even during the event where people look like they are having a great time, they may not be having that great of a time. "The reason we struggle with insecurity is because we compare our behind-the-scenes with everyone else's highlight reel," states Steve Furlick, who is a pastor, songwriter, and *New York Times* best-selling author.

Considering that we partly use social media to get attention, our feelings can be hurt when attention isn't received. We can misconstrue attention as self-worth. When our posts do not receive a lot of likes, we feel rejected and our self-worth can take a hit. The reality is that the number of likes you receive does not equate success. Social media can begin as a harmless habit and can become an obsession and a habit focused on the self. This habit can negatively influence our self-worth and the way we perceive others. When we are simply content to be ourselves and not compare or compete, we will be much more likely to gain the respect of others.

Our self-esteem can be influenced negatively when social media is disrupting to real-life thoughts and interactions. If watching what is going on in others' lives is affecting your thoughts and feelings about yourself, then it is harmful to your self-esteem. People get stuck on looking thin, attractive, or being involved in this or that activity, and it can cause them to be self-conscious. It is harmful to your self-esteem if it causes difficulty in face-to-face interactions with others. We have to admit that it is easier to text something than to state something face-to-face, especially with difficult conversations. How often do we use the easy way out of conversations by either texting or putting it on Facebook, Snapchat, or any other form of social media? Social media makes us believe that we are making social connections with others, but it is not built on real-life exchanges. Friends online can give us a false reality that they are close to us, even if they really are not. When people obsess with online interactions exclusively, they are missing out on hanging out with friends and family, doing fun things, getting involved in a hobby, or enjoying outdoor activities.

Do you compare your profile with others?

Does this comparison make you feel less than the other person?

Do you evaluate whether you are popular by how many likes or followers you have?

Do you spend a lot of time on social media and feel that it is not helping you to be your best or feel confident in yourself?

THREE

CAREER, JOB, AND TITLES

How does your job or career affect your self-esteem? The world definitely makes judgments based on what you do for work or what type of occupation you have. When you hear about different lines of work, what comes to mind? For a minute, think about this list of jobs: surgeon, school bus driver, CEO, cafeteria worker, accountant, garbage collector, computer technician, schoolteacher, janitor, factory worker, shoe salesman, chemist, mortician, professional sports player, entrepreneur, and nurse. What came to mind about the judgments we place on different jobs? What thoughts came to mind? The world has those judgments as well. The truth is that each job is acceptable as an occupation or position. My first job as a teen was at Taco Bell. I started by washing the bean pots and shining them. Then I moved to cutting black olives and finally moved up to the register. Even in one place of employment, there were varied levels of responsibility and job titles. I felt a lot better about myself at the register than scrubbing bean pots in the back room.

When we meet new people, we often ask a question about what they do for work. Think about conversations that people have when meeting someone new. "Hi. What's your name? What do you do for work? Oh wow. You're a doctor? That's impressive. What type of doctor are you?" Or another type of conversation could be "Hi. I'm Gertrude. What's your name? So what do you do for work? Oh. You work at Taco Bell?

Oh okay." The conversation ends, and the person moves on to someone else to converse with. Ever had a conversation like either of the above conversations? It can leave you feeling high or low based on others' reactions to your occupation. Reactions from others might make us feel fine about our jobs or feel insecure. Some people are in a transitional phase in their jobs, going to school, trying to figure out what they really want to do, are underemployed, or are maybe in jobs that aren't at their highest level of functioning. No matter what the situation is, one should not feel poorly about oneself because of what others think.

What others think about our jobs can influence our self-esteem and influence our own opinions of our jobs. Are you embarrassed to state what you do for a job because you aren't happy about it? Sometimes we think that we should be somewhere else in life, or we pictured ourselves in a better job or career by that stage. Maybe we are allowing our poor self-esteem to keep us from really pursuing our dream jobs or careers. Experts state that people with low self-esteem can subconsciously engage in behaviors that undermine their success, making them less likely to ask for or get promotions, raises, and even jobs. People with low self-esteem will often try to fly under the radar screen because they might not want to be noticed, so do not put themselves in a position to be promoted for higher positions. What's even worse is that low self-esteem may mask positive traits in an individual. We make assumptions about people who exhibit behaviors of low self-esteem and may interpret that they have lower intelligence, even though that may not be true. Those with lower self-esteem might not be risk-takers. They may not be the ones who will speak up in a meeting or take on challenging tasks. Low self-esteem also may display itself through body language or how one presents oneself. These behaviors may be displayed out of a fear of rejection. Whether it's the world's thoughts or our own thoughts about our jobs, it can without a doubt affect our self-esteem.

A job title is the level or position describing the responsibilities a person performs. Titles also describe the level of experience or expertise that an employee has. Think about the impact on someone's self-esteem when he or she has an impressive title behind his or her name. Think about these titles: CPA, CEO, CFO, and MD. What comes to mind about the individual who holds that position? We think, *Impressive,* right?

Management jobs use titles, such as manager, supervisor, director, or executive. We make a judgment about those in management as being more on the ball and probably making more money than those under their leadership. Job titles can be used to determine a career path and identify who might be up for a promotion. Some job titles in the business world are consultant, human resources, legal department, insurance, banker, administration, public relations, and purchasing salesman. Each of these titles holds a different weight and describes where we work. Some of the job titles in the creative industries might be social media manager, graphic artist, event planner, or fashion merchandiser. Service jobs require you to be able to communicate to a variety of people. Titles in the service jobs might be travel agent, restaurant manager, hospitality worker, real estate agent, and customer service representative. These service jobs support many of the conveniences that we enjoy. On-the-job training positions might have the titles of construction worker, transportation employee, manufacturer, and maintenance worker. The technical field has more of the high-end jobs. They require at least a four-year education. Technical job titles might be information technologist, science, environmental affairs employee, health care worker, Doctor, or engineer. Obviously, we might view the titles that require more education as being more impressive and providing more esteem. Titles in our society do influence our views of people as employees and as a result influence their self-evaluation.

Have you ever felt that others were judging you by your job, title, or career?

How do you feel about your occupation?

Are you content with your position, or do you really want to be doing something else?

Do you feel that you are using your God-given talents in your job?

Do you feel like your level of self-esteem is limiting you from going after a higher job?

FOUR

MONEY AND POSSESSIONS

We all have been caught up in wanting the next greatest thing. There is no better representation of this phenomenon than the Christmas shopping season. There are a million and one commercials for different products that you just can't live without! We are drawn to feeling that if we had these things, they would make us happy. A personal example happened when my husband and I went over to the house of one of his friends from college. He and his wife gave us a tour of their beautiful house. Granted, they have never had children. We were in the basement, where they showed us their movie theater room. Outside of that room was a real popcorn maker and a case with candy just like at the movies. When my husband and I left, I told him that I really liked the popcorn maker and candy case and added, "Wouldn't it be cool to have that?" He told me, "Yes, it would be cool to have, and we could have it if we didn't help our kids through college." That sort of put things in perspective. In life it didn't rate very high on the list of important things I needed. I also have had some dreams of purchases, such as a house with a wraparound porch on a lake with a boat and a horse in the backyard. Does my happiness depend on getting these material possessions? The answer is no. By the way, at this point in my life, I have none of the above dream purchases. The lack of these items does not affect my contentment.

So let's take a look to find out if money or possessions can increase your self-esteem. Companies for a long time have known that products that have an impressive name on them are a representation of status. Those who use or wear these products can be looked on more highly by their peers. What do you think about when you hear these expensive product names: Burberry, Cartier, Chanel, Rolex, Prada, Gucci, Armani, Dior, Louis Vuitton, Oscar de la Renta, Dolce & Gabbana, Ralph Lauren, Versace, or Giorgio Armani? We think of the words *luxurious, rich,* and *expensive* when we hear these names. What do you think when you see someone wearing anything with these names on them? We are impressed by that person and place a judgment that he or she is someone important or impressive.

I took a look at the luxury car business and found that the ten most expensive cars cost between $1.1 million and $3.9 million. Can you imagine having a car that expensive? The ten top car brands are Porsche, Jaguar, Maserati, Mercedes, Pagani, Aston Martin, Bentley, Rolls-Royce, Bugatti, and Maybach. If you drove up in one of those cars, you might feel really cool and important, even like a celebrity. Are you beginning to see how money can make people feel about themselves? If we owned the most expensive brands of clothes or cars, we might find that we would view ourselves more highly. Most of us drive something much different from those cars, and most of us do not wear the above brand names either. I'm content having a new used car that is five years old. I drive it the first month feeling like I have a pretty sweet ride!

Studies show that people do reap positive psychological benefits from purchasing high-status items. Some gain more benefits than others, but the studies state that it is unlikely the best way to boost your self-esteem. These purchases rev up the reward center of the brain, which is associated with a temporary rush of pleasure or good feeling, but they do not produce long-lasting satisfaction. When it comes to how much money you have, there are two extremes. On one extreme are individuals who don't have enough money to make ends meet or even to have a stable place to live. Having this type of deficit of money can weigh heavily on self-confidence. If your net worth is zero, it will affect how you see yourself, how confident you are, how you think, and how you act. There are many who struggle financially, whether it's difficulty in living month to month or having a specific financial strain, such as a health issue or school loans. On the other extreme are individuals who have so much money that they can buy the fanciest clothes, eat out whenever or wherever they desire, and own expensive luxury cars or airplanes. Having this much money might puff up your ego or make you feel powerful, but this extreme doesn't always lead to happiness. It seems like the best-case scenario financially to increase self-esteem would be to live in a happy medium—to have enough money to not be in debt and to live comfortably within one's means. You don't have to have a lot of possessions or expensive belongings to have self-confidence. When we moved from a small apartment into a new house that we built, I believed that I had just moved into the Taj Mahal. A Realtor who had much more money and a nicer house than I had told me that my house was a good "starter house." I believe that I could have been content living there for good. What a difference in standards. So why should someone who doesn't have as much as someone else not be content with what he or she has? When we compare ourselves to other people and their belongings, we become unhappy about what we have. Research shows that people are happier when they spend their money on life experiences as opposed to spending money on acquiring material possessions. Life experiences like vacations or outings are more likely to be experienced and enjoyed with others. This is partly why people are happier when they spend money on experiences and not on things. I have many great memories of vacations with my family to North Myrtle Beach, South Carolina. When we look at our pictures, we reminisce about those times and activities that we shared and how much fun we had! I would not look at a pair of pants or a shirt and reminisce about where I bought them. The pursuit of money remains a powerful motive among people of all income levels.

Unfortunately, all of us realize that we need money to eat and live. People commonly connect happiness with money. In a world where we value short-term pleasure, we equate spending money with happiness. People connect having money with having resources, being attractive to others, and having impressive social relationships. Sadly, using money as a social tool is the highest motivation and overall influence in the pursuit of accumulating money.

How much is money a motivator in your life?

Does the amount of money or possessions you possess affect how you feel about yourself?

Are you envious of others' things or the money they have?

FIVE

NATIONALITY AND ETHNICITY

Your nationality or ethnicity can affect how you see yourself and how the world sees you as well. In order to take an honest look at how nationality and ethnicity functions, we have to evaluate how our society views them both positively and negatively. There is no way to be comprehensive on this subject. An entire book on the topic would be more appropriate. When looking at ethnicity, there are some whose ancestors have been collected from different nationalities. My side of the family came over from England on the first couple of ships to America and intermarried with French, Germans, and American Indians. Needless to say, it is difficult for me to feel a connection to just one nationality. I often wished that there was something more ethnic about my side of the family. There aren't traditions that originated from my ethnic background. Whereas on my husband's side of the family, his mom's parents moved to the United States from Norway. His dad is partly Norwegian as well. Because their arrival to the United States was more recent, they have a deeper sense of their nationality as well as cultural traditions.

What does your culture, nationality, and ethnicity tell you about who you are? Your family has taught you beliefs about your heritage. How has that influenced you? It is interesting to look at some general common characteristics of different nationalities. In the world, there are 195 nations.

That simply means that there are endless combinations of ethnicities, each of them different from the others. The ethnic categories are Hispanic or Latino, White and European, Black and African, Asian, Native American and Alaska Native, and Native Hawaiian and other Pacific Islander. We will explore some common characteristics of the ethnic categories found in research and from professionals who have studied them. Because there are accommodation and assimilation, some of these shared characteristics may no longer be evident.

Accommodation is the concept where people from one country move to another country and incorporate the new information and the ways of the new culture into their established culture without losing some of their own differences. Assimilation is what happens over time if an ethnic group or individual does not hold to their country's differences but becomes like the people of the country that they have moved into. I have met and worked in counseling with clients from other countries. My first question is where they are from. The second question is to find out how long they have been in the United States. If their parents moved here and they were born here, then you see more of US styles, speech, and dress. If they were born out of this country, then I would need to understand their cultural differences.

Research states that Native Americans traditionally have respected the unique individual differences among people. They commonly express values, including staying out of others' affairs and verbalizing personal thoughts or opinions only when asked. They value attitude, behavior, and mutualism that permeate everything in the traditional American Indian social fabric. Mutualism promotes a sense of belonging and oneness with group members cooperating to gain group security and consensus. Traditional American Indians are involved in tribal relations that allow them to have a deep understanding of who they are and how they relate to the world around them.

When we explore the culture in India, studies have found a lack of privacy mainly from the numbers of people on the streets and in the communities. Because of the vast numbers of people in their communities, Indians tend to be very people oriented. Success is often achieved by the whole group advancing together. Importance is placed on knowing one's place. At social gatherings, they know where they are seated and where they rank within that status. I have known clients and church members who have had arranged marriages, which is a common practice. Those who come to the United States often still have events with other Indian families who celebrate their traditions together. There is an inherent connection to their culture and to others who have the same beliefs.

Being Hispanic is an ethnic distinction and originates from numerous countries that have differing physical traits and is found to be the largest ethnic minority. Hispanics share a common language but have different cultures, values, and beliefs. Research shows their commonalities are strong belief in fate and being tolerant and sympathetic to others as well as having close family ties and a connection to extended family. They are more flexible with time, and celebrations and entertainment always include food. Families often live with extended family members. Hispanic parents tend to show greater intimacy, protective behaviors, and strictness with their children. Their family ties help individuals to feel connected.

Asian cultures have a strong sense of respect and courtesy. They value the importance of respecting their elders, and behavior often is controlled by etiquette and the controlling of one's emotions. To display anger or impatience is a sign of weakness and shows a lack of mental strength. Maybe you've heard of the concept of saving face, which is supported by the community and is crucial in their societies. "Face" is equal to honor. If someone loses this, that person is viewed negatively, and he or she can find it difficult to gain back. Asians are defined as having a shame-based society. One's self-esteem is based more on others' views.

Another ethnic group is Eastern Europeans, who share the characteristic of toughness. Because of communism, wars, and winters, they have been defined as being intense, gritty, and sturdy people. They often endure difficulties or challenges with stoic determination. Some believe that they have better balance between work and play than most Americans. Those characteristics might allow them to have a stronger self-concept because of their strong will.

In the African countries, the self isn't separated from the community. One person's actions affect the community. African culture is based on the past and the present, which is why they respect their elders. Time is viewed differently when compared to other cultures, as they feel that scheduled times cannot be rushed. Because they often share homes with many family members, they are not uncomfortable being close to each other. Religion is a powerful force in their traditions and allows them to have a deep understanding of their ancestors.

What if diverse individuals were to converse with one another about their experiences? I guarantee their thoughts, experiences, and views would be different from one another. Let's say a Japanese, Hawaiian, South African, Bolivian, Australian, Russian, Irish, Brazilian, and Canadian were to discuss their experiences growing up. If they discussed what their cultures teach and what their life experiences in school, pleasurable activities, and traditions were like, you can imagine that their life experiences would be different and would influence their overall opinions and feelings about themselves. There are numerous ways that nationality and ethnicity affect the different cultures' self-esteem. Where a person is from and how long a person has been in the United States all influence an individual's self-view.

Do you know where your ancestors are from and what countries they originated from?

How has that influenced your worldview and how you fit into that view?

What experiences, either positive or negative, have you faced because of your ethnicity or culture?

Are you proud of your ethnicity? How does this influence your view of yourself?

SIX

VIEW OF SOCIETY

The definition of society is "a body of individuals living as members of a community". According to Dictionary.com, that "societal community contains an organized group of people who are associated together for religious, benevolent, cultural, scientific, political, patriotic, and other reasons". Culture consists of the "beliefs, behaviors, objects, and other characteristics common to the members of a particular group or society". Through culture, "people and groups define themselves, conform to society's shared values, and contribute to society. Culture may include customs, values, norms, rules, technologies, products, organizations, and institutions (ThoughtCo., "So What Is Culture Exactly?"). Culture and society are closely related. Most of us never consider how these things affect the way we see ourselves.

Our view of society, and what we believe about it, affects how we see ourselves in that society. Our world has changed. Shootings, mass murders, terrorism, abuse of children, countries at war, and people fleeing their countries are all the traumatic occurrences that we hear on the news, see in social media, or read in the newspapers. These traumatic situations may make us feel unsure of what is happening in the world and what life will be like in the future. Recently, people have even been complaining about those running for political office. We don't seem to like any of the choices. Where are all the honest, reputable public servants who could run our country in a God-fearing way? It could begin to make us question how we really fit in this world or how we can make a difference in spite of the bleak forecast of where the world is headed.

Racism in our society affects us profusely. In Charlottesville, the attack on those protesting against a white supremacist group that was spreading hate toward any group not white was heinous. A white supremacist ran his car through a crowd of protestors against them, killing one and injuring others. This type of hatred injures us as humans. Most people believe that there should be equality, and they stand up against bigotry and prejudice. They believe that all people were created equal. The few who don't believe this have created havoc with their hatred. I know that there are individuals in all nationalities that stand up against these radicals.

Since I think that I have presented more than my share of negative events in our society, here are some positive things that are happening. Although we have heard some negativity centered around Veterans Affairs, veteran homelessness has dropped 50 percent since 2010. There are a lot of great programs being offered to veterans that are taking care of many needs both physically and emotionally. The graduation rate is at an all-time high with all the nationalities, including African American, Hispanic, and Native American, and other groups such as low-income, disabled, and English-learning students, with an 83 percent overall graduation rate. There is also an all-time low of teen pregnancies. Obviously, this is extremely positive, as teens are not ready for parenting, and it decreases the number of single moms. The Americas are finally measles-free. What was once a disease that plagued the United States for many years has now been eradicated.

There are important characteristics for a society to function well, as stated in an article called "Society: 12 Most Important Characteristics of a Society." Likeness is the most important characteristic. If there isn't likeness, then there is no acknowledgment of belonging together. On the most basic level, we can acknowledge that we are all human, want to be treated fairly and to thrive in the activities we pursue. On the other side, differences are just as important as we become aware of, acknowledge, revel in, and learn about each other's differences. Interdependence is another important characteristic. We rely on each other for the parts we each play in society. We rely on others for shelter, food, and all the other conveniences in our day-to-day lives.

If we were to create our own society, a sort of utopia, what would we include? What if we each got to use our own creativity to come up with new innovations and ideas? I would like to see unity in the way we act equally toward others as well as respect for each other's ideas. What would your ideas of utopia look like? We all realize that we live in an imperfect world with imperfect people. Your thoughts about the world do affect how you feel about yourself. What your worldview is and how you see yourself in our society affect your self-concept and how you act as well.

What do you believe about society?

How do you see yourself fitting into your view of society?

Can you still believe the best about people?

Are you able to trust others you don't know? Do you find yourself distrusting everyone, including those you're close with? Or would you place yourself somewhere in the middle?

SEVEN

IQ, EQ, AND EDUCATION

IQ is based on intelligence, including how we learn and how well we perform on logical reasoning, word comprehension, abstract and spatial thinking, and math skills. As we all know, our intelligence affects our school performance and the grades we receive. Think of how important our grades were when we were in school. Tests were used to evaluate how well we knew the information taught in each of our classes. If you didn't get good grades or rate high on test scores, people wondered how smart you were. The whole academic process is based on performance of tasks, our ability to learn, and how quickly we learn. For a long period of time, IQ was thought to be the highest measure of success in life and career. Those with a high IQ show strength at work in taking on challenging tasks, possessing the ability to analyze, and finding connections.

How did you do in school, and how did you perform on grades and tests? How did your school performance affect how you viewed yourself? Maybe you were one of those students who never had to study, had a photographic memory, and aced all the tests. I think that we could all say that such a person is gifted with intelligence. Possibly you were one of those students who worked very hard and did well in classes. We are impressed by these students' intelligence as well. What about those students who try really hard and still struggle with tests and grades? Those who were embarrassed when they received their test scores or their report cards? Did you find yourself in any of these scenarios or somewhere in between? How does what you, or others, think about your intelligence influence your self-worth? Here are some synonyms of *smart*: *clever, bright, intelligent, sharp, quick, able, brainy, brilliant, wise, alert, genius, whiz, capable, gifted, up to speed, ingenious,* and *adept.* How do these words make you feel? I think that we would all agree that we would like all these words to be used to describe us! How about the opposite of smart? These synonyms are *clumsy, dull, foolish, ignorant, lazy, slow, typical, unclever, sluggish, unskilled, dense, dopey, simple, thick skulled, airheaded, birdbrained, gullible, mindless, nitwitted, uninformed,* and *untaught.* None of us like any of these words to define us when it comes to how intelligent we are. Do you find yourself thinking any of these words define you? Do you use these words as self-talk to describe you? What do you think about how intelligent you are, and how does that influence your thoughts about yourself?

EQ, on the other hand, is emotional intelligence. It is validly being able to reason with emotions and the use of emotions to enhance thought. It reveals itself by having the ability to perceive, control, evaluate, and express emotions. Those who have high EQs use their emotions to think and to understand emotional meaning as well as read others' emotions accurately. EQ is often evaluated by how a person relates to others and has the ability to control his or her own emotions. EQ often stems from emotional awareness learned in childhood. A child who is encouraged in qualities like sharing, putting himself or herself in someone else's shoes (empathy), thinking of others, learning appropriate physical boundaries, and learning to work well with others (cooperation), develop higher EQ. Have you ever met someone who is so easy to talk to and seems to understand what you are sharing with him or her? This would be someone who rates high on the EQ scale. Those who rate well are often good at teamwork, successful relations, and collaboration and are service oriented. Self-confidence is actually an important part of EQ. We might describe this person as someone who has his or her act together. Self-confidence is revealed by the belief that we can accomplish what needs to be done, even if we need to continue to work hard pushing past barriers.

Studies have proven that self-esteem affects a student's ability to learn and ultimately the level of education that one receives. "Healthy self-esteem is an essential component for learning. Regardless of age, the self-esteem of a learner facilitates or inhibits learning" (Solomon, 1992). Some teachers believe that at every learning stage has the potential to damage, maintain, or increase a student's self-esteem. In elementary students, we find that their evaluation of themselves is based on how a parent, teacher, or other important adult, such as a coach, views them. Can you think back to when you were in school and remember your favorite teacher? What was it about that person that made you appreciate him or her so much? Did he or she display material in a fun way, or did he or she like you or believe in you? Teachers clearly affect a student's learning, and their positive appraisal of the student over an extended time can actually increase a student's achievements. Teachers have found that low self-confidence in students may be displayed in learning problems, more missed days of school, behavioral issues, and susceptibility to sickness, as well as emotional and social problems. "Every success and failure, together with the reaction of peers, parents and teachers to these experiences, will contribute significantly to the student's self-worth, self-confidence, self-reliance and self-competence" (Robb and Letts, 1995).

So we find that there is an interconnection among IQ, EQ, and education. How we see ourselves in these categories affects how we feel about ourselves. Maybe we are incredibly intelligent, or maybe we are good at interacting with people and didn't do as well academically. Both of these categories affect the long-term success in school.

How has being smart or relatable affected your feelings toward yourself? What about your performance in school?

Have you let others define your abilities and how you rate how good you are?

What do you think that you could have achieved if you'd had better self-confidence?

EIGHT

BODY SHAPE AND LOOKS

How many of us when asked about what we think about our bodies come up with the negative first? Some complaints include, "I'm too tall, too fat, or too short"; "My hair is too thin"; or "My nose is too long." "If only my feet weren't so stubby, my hair so straight, and my eyes so close together, or if only I was prettier or better looking." If you make fun of yourself, you're not alone. It is hard to like everything about your body. When you get stuck on only thinking about the negative parts, it can really work on lowering your self-esteem. I'm embarrassed to say that I used to believe that all thin women were happier. Really? Obviously, this is an inaccurate fact, but I believed it nevertheless.

Body image is how you feel about your physical body. It can include how attractive you feel and how others view your looks. The specifics of body image are how we perceive our bodies visually, how we think and talk about our bodies, and our sense of others' thoughts about our bodies. Have you ever heard someone criticize another person's looks or even laugh at that person? That can make the person feel insecure about what others think of him or her. We may be tempted to believe that others are making fun of the way we look as well. With such strong societal scrutiny, it is easy to see how the focus on how we look can be more about the dark side of our negative body images. We have to take another look at what the media presents as the "perfect body." We often use these images as a comparison of how we should look. How often do we compare our looks to someone else we deem more beautiful, strong, and good-looking? The images of perfection we see in print, film, and television project an unrealistic version of reality that we are continually told is attainable. We think if we work out, eat less, and use expensive products to make our skin smooth and tight, then we can look that good. We are told that these unattainable bodies are normal, desirable, and achievable. When we don't measure up, we develop a strong distaste for our own looks. We have to know that the media images are photoshopped and edited to make them look more beautiful. These truths are often unspoken and taint our opinions of needing to look like the models or any famous person. The more that we focus and view the perfect images of others, and try to hold ourselves to those idealized characteristics, the worse we feel about ourselves.

Our families can have a positive or negative affect on the view we have of our bodies. Sometimes, parents and coaches can say harsh or critical statements about the weight of kids growing up. I have adult clients who are still insecure about their weight because of critical or mean statements they received as children from their parents. We can begin to believe what others have said about our bodies and take them on as our own beliefs. When a comment is made about our bodies, it can trigger our old beliefs from even childhood. This gives us an inaccurate view of what we really look like.

Women are typically unhappier than men in their view of their body image. Women are more apt to check the scales constantly. We all know heavier people who are happy and thin people who are not. Is size the biggest determination of a poor self-image? Maybe it's more about our own evaluation of what our bodies look like. You don't have to be thin to be attractive. We find that some of the opposite sex are looking for a nonperfect build. One of my roommates during my master's was Hispanic as was her boyfriend. He was attracted to substantial legs and large curves. I was caught off guard that he believed those features were beautiful. People of all different cultures can appreciate opposite features from other cultures. A poor opinion of your body can cause you to have lower self-confidence and can affect you by not presenting yourself confidently.

Men worry more about their height or how strong they are. Many men believe it would be worse to be short and thin with no muscles. Men's self-esteem is lowered when they don't fit the ideal stereotype of being strong, tall, and handsome. Men size one another up by looking at how strong they are or if they are good-looking or confident. They also compare themselves regarding the above issues as well.

There are aspects of poor body image that are concerning. Eating disorders are more common in women and can cause extreme health issues, including death. There are several eating disorders, such as bulimia, the overeating and vomiting of food. Another one is anorexia, which is the starving of oneself and often overexercising as well. The origin of these eating disorders stems from a person's inaccurate view of his or her body. Extreme plastic surgery also results from the dissatisfaction with one's looks. In the extreme form of this, it is called body dysmorphia. Focus is made on either minor or imagined flaws. People can spend hours daily trying to fix the flaw, or in the extreme cases, they can overuse cosmetic surgery. When they look in the mirror, they do not see an accurate picture. For men who want to look more muscular than other men, using steroids to help in bulking up muscles results in an extreme change in body shape. Men are looking for cut muscles and six-pack abs. The problem with all of the above issues, whether it is an eating disorder, overuse of cosmetic surgery, body dysmorphia, or the use of steroids, is that they are all harmful to our bodies and psyches. None of these methods are a positive way to deal with our negative image of our bodies.

I believe that as a society we are intolerant of body diversity in people's sizes and shapes. We as a society believe that being thin, muscular, and toned is associated with hardworking, respected, successful, popular, nice-looking, strong, and disciplined individuals. Being heavier is associated with being lazy, weak, unpopular, unsuccessful, and lacking willpower. So the association is not a description of a body characteristic but more about a moral character evaluation. Are those descriptions of others who might have different body sizes true? Positive image involves understanding that healthy, attractive bodies come in many shapes and sizes.

How would you describe your body shape and size?

How does your belief about your body affect how you feel about yourself?

Do you compare yourselves to others?

How does that make you feel about the evaluation of your self-worth?

NINE

ACTIVITIES AND TALENTS

The types of activities you participated in during childhood and into adulthood made an impact on the confidence level you developed. Maybe you were involved in horseback riding, dance, Boy Scouts or Girl Scouts, the student newspaper, youth group, sports, drama club, plays or musicals, or 4-H art classes. The choices of available activities are endless. Let's look at the impact of activities on a child's self-confidence first. Professor Margaret Talbot, president of the International Council for Sports Science and Physical Education, wrote that "sports, dance, and other challenging physical activities are distinctly powerful ways of helping young people learn to 'be themselves.'" She believed that physical activity helps children to move past the assumptions they might hold of their potential, and they might find that they have more potential than they thought. Self-esteem is developed by the confidence that arises from success in activities one is involved in. When children are successful in the activities they do, this can help them to believe that they can overcome challenges. If they are involved in a team activity, it can help develop close relationships as well as the feeling of being included. Physical activities can also help their view of their bodies. There are a number of studies that offer support to the claim that sports and other physical activities can contribute to the development of self-esteem.

Activities have been found to be helpful for those with learning disabilities, such as ADD or ADHD, and also help to keep kids in otherwise challenging environments out of trouble. Extracurricular activities help kids have positive social interactions and focus on things that they are interested in instead of focusing on their challenges. They get the opportunity to meet different types of people that they may have never had the chance to develop a relationship with otherwise. This widens their community network and builds self-confidence in interactions with others who may be different. Normally, there is some type of practice involved and discipline required in the activities. When they do well, it develops pride in their achievements, and they gain better self-respect, self-confidence, and self-esteem.

There are stereotypically more "cool" activities for youth, such as cheerleading, Key Club, football, and those in student government who decide what activities the whole high school will participate in. The weight of our perceptions of the activities we were involved in affects what type of self-confidence is gained from the participation in those activities. Honestly, as long as there were others who enjoyed and participated in those activities, there have to be positive feelings gained toward that activity.

Adults have the opportunity to be involved in varying types of activities and organizations that are different from children's activities. The categories of activities that are available are clubs and societies, leisure activities, volunteer opportunities, board participation, and professional and hobby organizations. When I looked up available organizations to participate in on the internet, there were 2,228! There is definitely something for everyone to be involved. Looking at a cross section of available things to be involved in under the category of hobbies, games, or sports, there were organizations, such as the National Wood Carvers Association, United States Chess Federation, United States Professional Tennis Association, International Rugby Board, American Folklore Society, American Humane Society, American Miniature Horse Association, United States Swimming, American Mensa, and Dance USA. I'm sure you are as surprised as I was by the wide variety of organizations. Whatever people are interested in, there is an activity open to them. Are some of the organizations meaningful to you or others in this category? We, as adults, have a lot of choices of clubs and organizations to be involved in.

Then there are professional organizations that may be helpful for those employed in those areas. A few of the organizations available to join are the American Society of Journalists and Authors, Association of Consulting Engineers, American Association of Occupational Health Nurses, American

Society of Travel Agents, American Association for Artificial Intelligence, National Association of Public Accountants, American Federation of Musicians, American Physical Therapy Association, American Society of Associates Executives, American Society of Media Photographers, National Association of Social Workers, the Geological Society, and the National Labor Relations Board. For those who are involved in these organizations, they can help to contribute to increased knowledge in their fields of practice and can be impressive to others who are aware of their participation. In the professional world, employers are also interested in what organizations and associations a potential or current employee is involved in.

Clubs are not just intended for children but also for adults. There are book clubs as well as clubs for cooking, tennis, arts and crafts, knitting, travel, volunteering, hiking, and many more. Engaging in social and productive activities that you enjoy can help to maintain well-being and contribute to higher self-confidence.

In childhood, what activities were you involved in?

How did those activities help you?

Have you ever had a positive or negative view of the activities that you chose to be involved in, either because of your own perception or from the perceptions of others?

Were there activities that you wished you had participated in?

Did you gain confidence from those activities?

In adulthood, how are the activities, clubs, or professional organizations that you are involved in affecting your view of yourself?

Does participation in those activities make you feel confident, important, or happy?

Do you feel like you are using your talents for God?

TEN

FRIENDS AND POPULARITY

What comes to mind when you think about the two concepts of having friends and being popular? Some of us think about other people we know now or knew in the past who were just those cool people everyone wanted to be friends with. Maybe you were that person or friends with that person. Then if it applied to your life situation, these concepts would emit positive emotions and memories. If you weren't that person, or friends with that cool person, then thinking about friends and popularity recalls negative emotions. Why are friends so important? We are going to find out whether having friends or being popular can or does affect our self-esteem.

We have found that there are high self-esteem types of friendships. These friendships are based on having mutual affection and respect, competition being low and support being high, having more positive than negative interactions, and disagreements leading to apologies. Friends can create good self-esteem when the friendship promotes closeness and connection, and they feel safe and comfortable around one another.

Quality relationships are important for our well-being and can have a big impact on our self-esteem. There is a protective impact on those who have friends. Meaningful friends can help protect each other through difficult life events and allow them to lessen the impact. Think of a time when you supported or were supported through a difficult life event, such as a death, loss of job, breakup of relationships, financial hardship, or conflict. If you had a close friend who was by your side supporting you all the way through the problem, then you realize how friends can protect us from more pronounced emotional reactions and an elongated time of struggling with the event. We all need friends—not just any friends but healthy, good ones. You may have heard it said that if you could count on one hand how many good, real friends you have, then you are a lucky person. On the opposite side, we find that those who have low self-esteem already make poor choices of friends. Those who have low self-esteem don't choose good friends, and those who don't have friends have lower self-esteem. We also find that those who do not have friends are judged more harshly by themselves and by others. They may be viewed as being outcasts or not likable. Some of the reasons why people may not have friends are many, such as in the process of making changes, being shy, letting go of unhealthy relationships, communication issues, perfectionism, or having strange personality habits. There are many in this world who do not have quality friendships. When you are excluded by others and lack friends, it can greatly influence your self-esteem. Feelings of inferiority, depression, resentment, and anxiety can develop and can lead to withdrawal from wanting to be around people. These are all negative, measurable impacts on the influence of having or not having friends.

Peers are people who are equal to one another in abilities, age, background, or something of equal worth or value. Peers can influence the type of person you become, which can affect how you feel about yourself. It is important to be aware of the type of people you are hanging out with and whether they are helping to bring the best out in you. In an ideal situation, both you and your friend know each other's value and treat one another with respect. If one of you has poor self-esteem, then the friendship gets unbalanced. Low self-esteem can cause you to choose the wrong type of people, have difficulty dealing with confrontation, and become codependent. If you choose friends who make poor choices, you may apt to become like them. But if we choose friends who inspire us to be our best and to reach our goals, then they could help us to do more amazing things. You're likely to start acting like the people you surround yourself with. Taking control of the influences in your life is the first step toward building self-confidence. It takes determination and an ability to look objectively at yourself.

Low self-esteem can make it difficult to forge new relationships. If you have the belief that you don't deserve good friends, then you might actually turn down opportunities to meet new people. I've heard more than my share of times that clients are sure that if people really knew them, then they would run and hide. They believe that inherently they are unlovable. This is a vicious cycle that just builds on itself. The best bet is to stop listening to the inner voice telling you that nobody wants to be your friend.

What are some positive aspects of relationships with friends? If you are struggling with willpower or being motivated, then a strong-willed person can help to bring self-discipline to your life. In a study in *Psychological Science* in 2013, it reported that when people are running low on self-control, they often seek out self-disciplined people to boost their willpower. So whether you are tempted to skip a workout or spend too much money, a disciplined friend can be helpful to maintain healthy habits. Another benefit of good friends is that it increases your longevity. This was found to be true in a study in 2005 conducted by Flinders University in Australia. They studied 1,500 older adults for ten years and found that those who had a larger network of friends outlived those who didn't by 22 percent. Having friends in one's older years may actually be the elixir of youth. There were other studies that found friendships can help lower blood pressure, cholesterol, and heart rate. It's amazing that having friends can have pronounced health benefits.

So what about popularity? When we look at the word *popular,* it means being liked, admired, or enjoyed by many people or by a particular person or group. Our first thought that may come to mind when thinking about being popular may take us back to our teens and high school. You may be tempted to think that the things that happened way back then are meaningless to our here and now. Dr. Mitch Prinstein is one of the world's foremost researchers on the psychology of popularity, and he says that the past does matter. He wrote a book called *Popular,* where he stated, "I believe that what we know is that people's status may change; their internal experience does not. The research shows that our brains are built and developed, we really pull on those old adolescent memories far more than we realize." He stated that there are two types of popularity. One is our social reputation or status, and the other one is social preference or likability. You might have both of these or just have one or the other. We would all like to be popular in both of these areas. If in high school you were one of those cool kids but people feared you, then you would be considered to have high status but low likability. How about if you were a geek but charming at the same time? Then you would have low status and high likability. Lastly, if you were someone who was friends with all kind of different groups and they all liked you, then you would have high status and high likability.

He found that those who had a tough time during the high school years struggle as adults as well. It's not the only variable for the future success. The way to overcoming your past is to come to terms with who you were and then move forward, focusing on who you are currently. Prinstein said that likability is one of "the most valuable social commodities" in our society. You have to learn to invest in likability as much as you invest in other areas. The groups in your life currently, such as work, neighborhood, church, social functions, or any clubs or organization you may find, you rate differently in popularity. As you focus on being a good friend and a good influence on others, it will boost your self-confidence.

Would you consider yourself to be someone with a lot of friends or someone who struggles making friends?

Are you someone others like to spend time with?

Do you consider yourself a good friend?

Do you surround yourself with healthy people?

Have you ever considered yourself popular?

If you weren't popular in the past or currently, how has that affected your view of yourself?

WORLD'S INFLUENCE ON SELF-ESTEEM

Identify your own

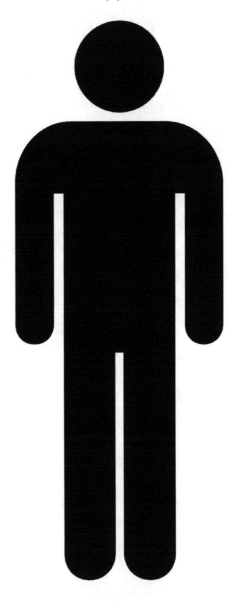

World's Influence on Self-Esteem: Identify Your Own

As we make the transition from looking at the world's influence to how God sees us as we really are, there are some incredible scriptures that help us understand why we shouldn't listen to the world. The Bible is so amazing because it speaks truths that only it can express. So in the next section, you will see these scriptures written out. They are so clear in their message, and we cannot understand them unless we read them. I encourage all of you to read the scriptures multiple times and even meditate on them. These scriptures are the key to really learning and accepting the important truths of who you really are! John 5:44 states, *"How can you believe if you accept praise from one another, yet make no effort to obtain the praise that comes from the only God"* (italics mine). We need to be more concerned about what God thinks instead of trying to get the praise from people. First John 5:5 tells us, *"Who is it that overcomes the world? Only he who believes that Jesus is the Son of God"* (italics mine). This is how we put behind us the influence of the world.

We can overcome the world if we believe and imitate Jesus. He experienced a lot of stress and persecution from the world. His focus was only on pleasing God. Thus, if we want to put away the influences of the world, we must focus only on what God thinks of us—an audience of one. In 1 Corinthians 3:19, it says, "For the *wisdom of this world is foolishness in God's sight*" (italics mine). The world's thoughts are foolish to God. So we would be wise to be concerned about God's opinion. Jeremiah 17:5, 7 states, "This is what the Lord says: *'Cursed is the one who trusts in man who draws strength from mere flesh and whose heart turns away from the Lord. But blessed is the one who trusts in the Lord, whose confidence is in Him'"* (italics mine).

We are blessed if we trust in God and His thoughts about us. God discourages us from looking at our own flesh to find our stability and confidence. Galatians 1:10 says, *"Am I now trying to win the approval of men, or of God? Or am I trying to please men? If I were still trying to please men, I would not be a servant of Christ"* (italics mine). If we are God's people, then we should try to please God and not look to get the approval of humankind. People's opinions change like the shifting sand, but God's opinion never changes. His promises are constant and we can be sure in them.

—————— PART 2 ——————

GOD'S VIEW OF YOU

To understand self-esteem God's way is to comprehend deeply that He knows every breath we take and how many hairs are on our heads. He knows our thoughts and what we will say before the words come out of our mouths. He has plans for you and puts you in the exact places that you should live. He is such a personal, intimate God who is to be loved and who loved us before we were in existence and had a deep knowledge of who we would be. This is the God who thinks we are special, unique, important, and of royalty. Isn't it much more important to know what the God who created us thinks about us? We wouldn't even be on this planet without Him, so what we think about ourselves is enveloped in our Creator and His thoughts about us. Now the work begins to change how you think about yourself. Come explore and challenge yourself to understand not just mentally but in your heart what God wants you to feel about you!

God makes us radiant, shining, at peace, secure, strong, unashamed, great, heard, confident, helped, sustained, loved, comforted, forgiven, blessed, able, gloried, victorious, guarded, shining brightly, prosperous, honored, not weary, soaring like eagles, feel paths are smooth, engraved on God's hands, carried, rescued, summoned by name, a title of honor, precious, formed and made, hopeful, listened to, conquerors, content, powerful, self-disciplined, unfailing kindness, power made perfect in weakness, breathed by God, in God's image, cared for, rulers over creation, kept firm, fellowship in Christ, mind of Christ, coworkers in God's service,

God's building, God's temple, and sacred temple. You have to start back in Genesis to see what God stated when He created humankind. "This was good."

We need to ask ourselves if we are actively seeking to find out what God wants us to see. As it says in Psalm 53:2, "*God looks down* from heaven on the sons of men *to see if there are any who understand, any who seek God*" (italics mine). Let's seek out God's plans for us and understand and accept how He wants us to feel about ourselves.

I love the Casting Crowns song about listening to the world or listening to the voice of truth, which is from God. We tell ourselves the world's untruths and it limits us from reaching our full spiritual potential. Listen to the song "Voice of Truth." This song helps us to focus on God's voice and not on the world's.

GOD'S INFLUENCE ON SELF-ESTEEM

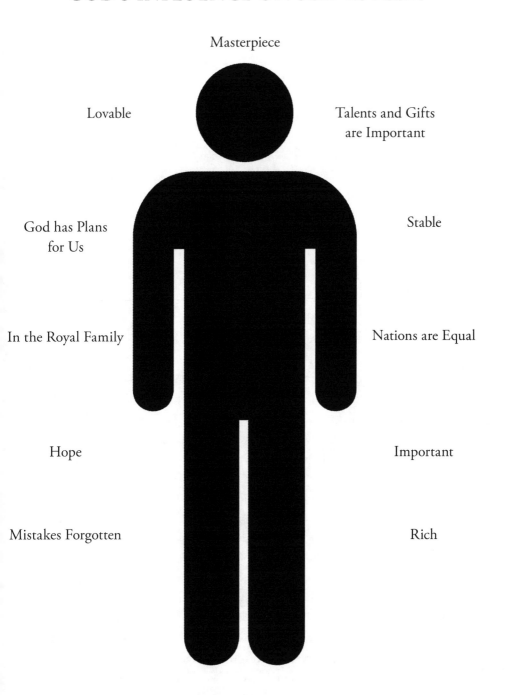

Masterpiece

Lovable

Talents and Gifts
are Important

God has Plans
for Us

Stable

In the Royal Family

Nations are Equal

Hope

Important

Mistakes Forgotten

Rich

ELEVEN

GOD CREATED YOU
A MASTERPIECE

God created gazillions of stars and called them all by name. He set in motion all the planets and galaxies yet is interested in the finite details of our lives. He even knows the very number of hairs on our heads. Matthew 10:30 tells us this: "And even the very *hairs on your head are numbered*" (italics mine). Even with the realization that the number of our hairs change every day, He still is attentive to keeping the accurate number. He was involved in the details of our lives even before we were born. He called us and created us with our own set of characteristics, talents, and personalities, just as He planned. We bring glory to Him as we use our own special ways for Him. Colossians 1:16 tells us, "For in Him all things were created: things in heaven and on earth, visible and invisible, whether thrones, or powers or rulers or authorities; *all things have been created through Him and for Him*" (italics mine).

In order to begin the study of how God views us, we have to start with man's conception. We need to start at the beginning. Genesis 2:7 says, "Then the Lord God formed a man from the dust of the ground and *breathed into his nostrils the breath of life*, and the man became a living being" (italics mine). Can you believe that we have God's very breath of life in us? The Creator breathed into us the His own breath and our life began. And in Genesis 1:27, it states, "So *God created mankind in His own image,* in the image of God He created them; male and female He created them" (italics mine). We were created in His image! We are the direct representation of our Creator. We each have specific and different characteristics of God in us. In the book *Beautiful Lies,* written by Jennifer Strickland, she shares, "Before the fall, Eve's worth was embedded in God alone, both she and Adam looked to him as a measure of their value. God provided all they needed; he was more than enough."

She also shared a story about her mother that helps to understand how God feels about all our imperfections.

> My mother knits. With my first child … Mom knit an intricately designed baby blanket for her. She used two spools of delicate yarn for each stitch. She also used a variety of pastel colors to create a pattern of blocks in the blanket. Mom worked her fingers to the bone knitting that blanket, and when she gave it to me, it was soft and pretty and made with so much love. But it wasn't perfect. The blocks hung a little lopsided when I held the blanket up in the light. Over the years I nursed Olivia in that blanket. I tucked her in at night in that blanket. And when she got older, she dragged the blanket through the house and up and down the stairs.

This is how God views our imperfections. He uses us with all our imperfections and allows us to be beautiful and loved. Even though we are lopsided and incomplete, He still loves us. He loves us enough to fill in the areas that are incomplete. If our mothers had made a blanket, we wouldn't have found ourselves saying that the quilt wasn't perfect or that we didn't want it. We wouldn't have explained that we really wanted a different type of blanket or one that was better looking or perfect. That quilt became dearly loved and used by the child without their knowledge of its imperfections.

Do we ever inadvertently say to God that we wish He had knitted us together differently and that we are not satisfied by his work? Psalm 139:1–3, 5, tells us, "O, Lord, you have searched me and you know me. You know when I sit and when I rise; you perceive my thoughts from afar.

You discern my going out and my lying down; you are familiar with all of my ways. ... You hem me in-behind and before; you have laid your hand upon me."

In verses 13–14, 16, it tells us how God knitted us together. "For *you created my inmost being; you knit me together in my mother's womb.* I praise you because *I am fearfully and wonderfully made*; your works are wonderful ... *All the days ordained for me were written in your book before one of them came to be*" (italics mine). He knit us together just as He wanted us to be. We are each a knitted quilt masterpiece. We are all carefully crafted by our Maker in a wonderfully ornate blanket. Each blanket is to be marveled by others and cherished by God. Psalm 119:73 states, "*Your hands made me and formed me*; give me understanding to learn your commands" (italics mine). If we thoroughly understand what our worth is to God, then we would understand who we are. We were carefully crafted by God to be the very special, unique person that we are.

The world is apt to look at the outward appearance, yet God sees so much more in us. In 1 Samuel 16:7, it says, "But the Lord said to Samuel, '*do not consider his appearance or his height,* for I have rejected him. The Lord does not look at the things man looks at. *Man looks at the outward appearance, but the Lord looks at the heart*" (italics mine). Samuel had come to Jesse's house because God told him that he'd find the one who would be anointed the next king. Samuel had Jesse's seven sons, starting from the oldest down, pass in front of him. None of them were the right one to be anointed. Samuel asked if he had any other sons. The youngest son was tending the sheep. Samuel waited for David to come in from the pasture and anointed him the next king to replace Saul. David was the least of the sons in his family as he was the youngest. Yet scripture tells us that David was a man after God's own heart.

God looks at the inner qualities of strength and sees us as royalty as well. A later chapter will focus solely on being royalty. Psalm 18:16 states, "He reached down from on high and took hold of me; He *drew me out of deep waters*" (italics mine). God believes in us so much. He reaches down and takes a hold of us and brings us out of unsafe places. In verse 19, it states, "He brought me out into a spacious place; *He rescued me because He delighted in me*" (italics mine). God delights in me? I believe that He delights in me because He created me in a way that brings Him pleasure and glory. It's amazing that our Creator even considers us at all, let alone reaches us in the happy and dark places.

God marks His name on us. Isaiah 49:16 tells us, "See, I have *engraved you on the palms of my hands*; your walls are ever before me" (italics mine). What do you think He marks on the palm of His hands? Maybe He writes all the blessed names that He calls us by. Or He might write His love for us, ways He protects us, or marks us as His own. God is possessive of us. He believes in us and loves when we understand our worth to Him.

Have you ever heard a proud parent describe their child as the apple of their eye? Well, God has us as the apple of His eye. Psalm 17:8 says, "*Keep me as the apple of your eye*; hide me in the shadow of your wing" (italics mine). Also found in Zechariah 2:8, it states, "For whoever touches you touches the apple of His eye" (italics mine). Wow. God is like a proud parent where He tells us that we are important enough to be the apple of His eye! There are times that we feel we are not doing well spiritually. We can be tempted to believe that God isn't proud of us or that He wouldn't brag about us. Being the apple of His eye is not about our greatness but about God loving His creation.

As if being the apple of God's eye wasn't enough, He tells us more about His feelings. Psalm 8:3–5 states, "When I consider your heavens, the work of your fingers, the moon and the stars, which you have set in place, *what is man that you are mindful of him, the son of man* that you care for him? You made him a little lower than the heavenly beings and crowned *him with glory and honor*" (italics mine). We wonder why God is mindful of us or why He would care for us. He tells us His thoughts, which include that He placed us a little lower than the heavenly beings. So we are being compared to angels. Then He goes even further and tells us that He crowns us with glory and honor. God wants us to fully understand our worth in His eyes. The angels have been placed here to help us get to heaven. Hebrews 1:14 says, "Are not all *angels ministering spirits sent to serve those who will inherit salvation?*" (italics mine). God sends His heavenly beings to serve us! That is how high His thoughts are regarding us.

God tells us that we are His temple and that His Spirit is in us. First Corinthians 3:16–17 tells us, "Don't you know that *you yourselves are God's temple and that God's Spirit dwells in your midst?* If anyone destroys God's temple, God will destroy that person; for God's temple is sacred, and you are that" temple (italics mine). What ways do you not treasure your bodies as God's temple where He lives? There are many ways that we don't take care of our own bodies because we don't truly understand how important our houses of God are. He says that we are the holy temples where He chooses to live. We need to live lives that are worthy of His presence in our bodies.

We are told that God is interested in us as His creation from conception until we are old and gray. Isaiah 46:3–4 states, *"You whom I have upheld since you were conceived and have carried since your birth. Even to your old age and gray hairs I am he,* I am He who will sustain you and I will carry you; I will sustain you and I will rescue you" (italics mine). We are created by Him in our mother's womb, and we are just as treasured of a possession in our old age. He still sees us as His blessed creation. There are times that we just don't feel all that much like a masterpiece. Ecclesiastes 3:11 says to us, "He has made everything beautiful in its time. He has also set eternity in the human heart; yet no one can fathom what God has done from beginning to end." This says it all.

Satan wants you to believe this: You are ordinary and faulty and will amount to nothing.

This is who you are: A special created being who is different from everyone else—perfect in every way.

Listen to the song by Danny Gokey called "Masterpiece."

Do you believe that you are a masterpiece?

If you struggle believing this, why?

Have you felt that God made a mistake on some part of you?

Do you understand that He created you just as He wanted to?

Do you think often about how God is attentive to every detail of your life?

How would you act if you truly understood that you were God's temple?

TWELVE

WE ARE LOVABLE

Most of us have at times not felt that lovable. We realize that we all have qualities that are not lovable and push others away. Yet God tells us that He still chooses us. 1 Thessalonians 1:4–5 states, "For we know, *brothers and sisters loved by God,* that *He has chosen you*, because our gospel came to you not simply with words but also with power, with the Holy Spirit and deep conviction" (italics mine). We are God's children loved and chosen by Him! Not because of anything lovable in ourselves but because of who He is. Even in our unlovable moments, He still loves us! Sit and think hard about this concept. There is nothing that you can or cannot do that changes the outright fact that He chooses to love us. We are not loved by God by our own awesomeness but by His greatness. God's love is always unconditional and amazing.

How long will God love us? We wonder if He will stop loving us at some point. We wonder if He might become tired of us because we are not spiritually impressive. Deuteronomy 7:9 answers this question: "Know therefore that the Lord your God is God; He is the *faithful God, keeping His covenant of love to a thousand generations* of those who love Him and keep His commandments" (italics mine). How long He will love us and our families is for a thousand generations. The only requirement is that we love Him and follow His Word. He will love us for thousands of years if we show our love and commitment to Him, even imperfectly. That's all that God has ever wanted from us. He created us and loved us hoping that we would return His love. He loves you so much that He was willing to sacrifice His Son. John 3:16 states, "For *God so loved the world that He gave his one and only Son,* that whoever believes in Him shall not perish but have eternal life" (italics mine).

Would you sacrifice one of your children to a world that might not even care about your sacrifice? That is exactly what God did when He sent Jesus. He knew that we might not accept who He was or the sacrifice they both made. God came in flesh from heaven to a sinful world. Wow. He loves us that much! Psalm 117:1–2 says, "Praise the Lord, all you nations; extol him all you peoples. For *great is his love towards us,* and the faithfulness of the Lord endures forever" (italics mine). God's love for us is great. We can be assured of how long we will be loved by God—forever!

What is the magnitude of God's love for us, and could we ever be separated from His love? We wonder if we ever truly understand how deep His love is. Ephesians 3:17–19 tells us, "I pray that you, *being rooted and established in love,* may have power, together with all of the saints, to *grasp how wide and long and high and deep is the love of Chris*t, and to know *this love that surpasses knowledge*—that you may be filled to the measure of all the fullness of God" (italics mine). His love surpasses our ability to comprehend. This is because we cannot visualize the parameters of the width, length, or depth of God's love for us. This type of love fills us up and helps us to experience His fullness. We can be filled by His love in ways that we cannot even comprehend. Psalm 103:11 says, "For a*s high as the heavens are above the earth, so great is his love* for those who fear him" (italics mine). There is no way to be aware of the distance from the earth to heaven. Yet He loves us all the way from heaven. All these scriptures express concepts beyond our understanding of His greatness. So we are given these visual reminders that His love is immeasurable.

Can we trust in God's love? We have difficulty understanding something that we cannot see, such as God or His love. Some people have been hurt in relationships and as a result have trust issues. They wonder if God might be like others who have let them down. God tells us in Jeremiah 31:3, "The Lord appeared to us in the past, saying, '*I have loved you with an everlasting love;* I have drawn you with unfailing kindness'" (italics mine). We don't have to fear being hurt by Him. God tells us that

He will love us with everlasting love. This is a love that we can put our trust in. Our response to this type of love is found in Psalm 13:5–6: "But *I trust in your unfailing love*; my heart rejoices in your salvation. I will sing to the Lord, for *He has been good to me*" (italics mine). The way that we can trust in His love is to remember how good God has been to us. We have reminders of His blessings every day. We need only to be cognizant of them and acknowledge them.

Sometimes our hearts and minds need to be examined to see if we are focusing on the right things. We can lose sight of what God's love is really like and get bogged down by thoughts of worldly issues. Psalm 26:2–3 says, "Test me, O Lord, and try me, examine my heart and my mind; for *your love is ever before me*, and I walk continually in your Truth" (italics mine). What should our hearts and minds be focused on? We should just "park out" on the amazing truth that God's love is ever before us. Another reminder of what our hearts should focus on is in 2 Thessalonians 3:5, 13: "May the *Lord direct your hearts into God's love* and Christ's perseverance. And as for you, brothers, never tire of doing what is right" (italics mine). We need help and direction to see God's love and understand it. The truth is that He is always thinking about us and our well-being. He wants the best for us. Even during difficult times, He wants to give us that gentle reminder—that we are loved. "The Lord delights in those who fear Him, who *put their hope in His unfailing love*" (Psalm 147:11; italics mine).
Satan wants you to believe this: You are not lovable and no one will ever love you for who you are.

This is who you are: Loved in every way and lovable and loved by God more than you can comprehend, even during difficult times.

Listen to the song by Tauren Wells called "Known."

Do you ever question God's love for you?

What gets in the way of feeling or believing in God's love?

Do you think that God will tire of you and decide that you are not lovable?

What do you need to help remind you of God's love for you?

THIRTEEN

OUR TALENTS AND GIFTS
ARE IMPORTANT

Give God thanks for all He has given you. He gives us talents that we are born with, and when we become His children, we are given spiritual gifts. He has blessed each of us with a special talent or talents and gifts. Your talent or gift can be your unique personality, your ability to give kind words, musical ability, giving, preaching, speaking wisdom, compassion, teaching skills, charisma, communication skills, planning big events, financial skills, or any other area that you're good in. There are endless gifts that God has blessed us with. Maybe you wonder if you really have a talent or if your talent is all that important. Everyone has a gift or talent that can be used to edify the group of believers. Maybe you have placed more importance on some gifts than others. Some are tempted to think that the full-time minister or others who serve in more public roles are more important. Let's see what God says about that concept. In 1 Corinthians 1:7, it says, "Therefore *you do not lack any spiritual* gift as you eagerly wait for our Lord Jesus Christ to be revealed" (italics mine). We do not lack any spiritual gift. I'm pretty sure this message was for everyone. We all have spiritual gifts. James 1:17 tells us, *"Every good and perfect gift is from above,* coming down from the Father of the heavenly lights, who does not change like shifting shadows" (italics mine). God is the one who gives us our gifts. If you are unsure of your spiritual gift or gifts, there are resources that allow you to identify them. One resource is a book called *Discover Your God-Given Gifts* by Don and Katie Fortune. It is a good way to help you to extensively explore your gifts. Another resource is a book called *Finding Your Spiritual Gifts* by C. Peter Wagner. God thinks that your talents and gifts are important and is just waiting for you to use them to bring Him glory. He has blessed each one of us with our own special talent that is different from everyone else's. He wants you to know what gift that He has blessed you with. If you are unsure of your talents, explore and discover them.

How should we use our gifts to edify the church and bring God glory? First Corinthians 12:4–6 says, "There are *different kinds of gifts,* but the same Spirit distributes them. There are *different kinds of service, but the same Lord.* There are *different kinds of working,* but in all of them and in everyone it is the same God at work" (italics mine). In verses 12–26, it tells us that we are a part of one body, and each part plays its part. Each part is just as important in its role of serving as all the other parts of the body. The eyes cannot tell the ear, "We don't need you." Each must do the work that the Lord determines for them. In verses 27–29, it says that there are gifts in teaching, healing, administration, and other fields. We each are a part of the body of Christ, and every part of the body is important and vital. Your gifts are as important as every part of the body. God tells us that sharing our gifts is vital.

How should we use our important talents? First Peter 4:9–11 states, "Offer hospitality to one another, *without grumbling.* Each one should *use, whatever gift he has received to serve others,* faithfully administering God's grace in its various forms. If anyone *speaks, he should do it as one speaking the very words of God.* If anyone *serves, he should do it with the strength God provides,* so that in all things, God may be praised through Jesus Christ. To him be the glory and the power for ever and ever. Amen" (italics mine). This states very clearly that whatever gifts we have been given, and we all have at least one, they are to be used to serve others. We should use our gifts in serving as if we are serving God and serve with the strength that God provides. He gives us the blessings of gifts, and then He also gives us the power to use them! I guess we have no excuse for not using our gifts.

Another scripture that lets us know how we should use our gifts is in Romans 12:6–8. It says, "*We have different gifts,* according to the grace given us. If a man's gift is *prophesying,* let him use it in proportion to his faith. If it is *serving,* let him serve; if it is *teaching,* let him teach; if it is *encouraging,* let him encourage; if it is *contributing to the needs of others,* let him give generously;

if it is *leadership,* let him govern diligently; if it is *showing mercy,* let him do it cheerfully" (italics mine). We are first told that we all have different gifts and that they are given to us by God's grace. We are called to use our gifts and to put them into practice. It's as if we were created to be used by God to serve in these ways. If we are not serving, then we are not expressing our gratitude for the gifts that we have been blessed with. Also, I'm very glad that we don't all have the same gifts, because it would be like we were all an eye or an ear. That would be a strange-looking body! We need every part of the body; therefore, we need every gift used in the body of Christ.

Should we practice and excel in the gifts that the Lord has given us? Exodus 35:10 says, "All who are *skilled* among you are to come and *make everything the Lord has commanded*" (italics mine). And in Proverbs 22:29, it says, "Do you see a *man skilled* in his work? He will serve before kings; he will not serve before obscure men" (italics mine). If our talents and gifts are from God, then we need to use our gifts and continue to excel until we are skilled in those areas. When we are skilled in using our talents for God, we can influence important people, even kings. We can use our talents to bring God glory even outside the church and have the ability to influence people to see God in us. We are expected to use the talents given to us by God, use them excellently, and to give our best.

God tells us that our talents and gifts are important. He gave us all our talents and blessed us all with different talents that are equally as important. Colossians 3:23–24 tells us, "Whatever you do, *work at it with all your heart as working for the Lord,* not for men, since you know that you will receive an inheritance from the Lord as a reward. It is the Lord Christ you are serving" (italics mine). Discover your gifts, and use them to serve as if you were serving God. We use our talents not to gain the praise from others but for the reward that we receive by God. We receive the gift of satisfaction when we use our talents and gifts and also the reward of an inheritance with God.

Satan wants you to believe this: You are not talented and have nothing to offer that would be helpful or appreciated.

This is who you are: Talented and gifted to be useful to God's plan to bring Him glory.

Listen to Matthew West's song called "Do Something."

Are you aware of the talents and gifts that God has given you?

How important do you think that your talents are to yourself or others?

Have you ever thought that your talents aren't as useful as others?

Are you using your talents and gifts that God has blessed you with?

Are you practicing and becoming more skilled in those talents?

FOURTEEN

GOD HAS PLANS FOR US;
WE CAN BE HIRED

We often wonder if God has specific plans for us. Can we be hired in His kingdom or in the employment world? If only we knew for sure what His plans were for us. Many of us like to be in control of the direction we are moving in. We can be tempted to try to take control of what we think is best for us or even what we think God's plans are. In Proverbs 16:9, it tells us how we should really view it: "In his heart a man plans his course, but *the Lord determines his steps*" (italics mine). God already has the greatest plans of all for us. Nothing that we could ever come up with in our own imagination or goal setting would be as great as His plans are for us. It's okay for us to write out goals, but we should do so in pencil so that God can help to determine where to lead us and where He wants us to land.

This next scripture helps us to understand this concept as well. Proverbs 16:25, says, "There is *a way that seems right to a man*, but in the end it leads to death" (italics mine). Sometimes we think that we know where we are headed, but only God knows and will lead us on the right path, when we listen to His voice. Psalm 4:3 states, *"Know that the Lord has set apart the godly for himself; the Lord will hear when I call to Him"* (italics mine). Bring your hopes and dreams to Him, and He will listen and lead you in the right direction to His plans!

When did God actually make what His plans were for us? Isaiah 25:1

says, "O Lord, you are my God; I will exalt you and praise your name, for in perfect faithfulness *you have done marvelous things, things planned long ago*" (italics mine). God has had a marvelous plan for us for a very long time. He has been thinking about our specific situations, and we can be assured that He has great plans for us. We can also be assured of how He is thinking about our futures. In Jeremiah 29:11, it says to us, "For *I know the plans I have for you*, declares the Lord; *plans to prosper you* and not to harm you, *plans to give you a hope and a future*, then you will call upon me and come and pray to me, *and I will listen to you.* You will seek me and find me when you seek me with all your heart" (italics mine). God wants us to understand that He desires for us to prosper. He tells us specifically that He knows the plans for us. He has our best interest in mind. He wants us to have a future that feels hopeful. But the only way to accomplish that is to call on God and pray to Him for His direction in our lives. We have to be wholehearted in our pursuit of Him. This is the only way to find His plans for us.

Does God actually hear our prayers? Second Chronicles 30:27 answers that question: "The priests and Levites stood to bless the people, and *God heard them, for their prayer reached heaven, His holy dwelling place*" (italics mine). Our prayers for the future and for what plans to pursue in work reach God's holy dwelling place. Psalm 4:3 tells us the same thing about God hearing us: "*Know that the Lord has set apart the godly for himself; the Lord will hear when I call to Him*" (italics mine). We can be assured that He loves to hear us ask Him for His direction in our plans! When we show God that we love Him and are interested in hearing about what His plans are for us and our futures, then we seek and understand His thoughts. It tells us in Romans 8:28–29, "And we know that in all things *God works for the good of those who love him, who have been called according to his purpose.* For those God foreknew he also *predestined to be conformed to the image of his Son*, that he might be the firstborn among many brothers and sisters" (italics mine). Can you believe that God works in our situations for our good? He also tells us that He has called us to a purpose. He already knew us and allowed us to be fashioned in and conformed to the likeness of Jesus. Surely that prepares us to be ready to do amazing things in our lifetimes and to be employees.

What type of employees or workers should we be? First Chronicles 28:9–10 tells us, "For the *Lord searches every heart and understands every desire and every though*t … Consider now, for the Lord has *chosen you* to build a house as the sanctuary. *Be strong and do the work*" (italics mine). He chooses us to be His workers, but He also searches our hearts and understands our desires and thoughts. He tells us that we should be strong in the way that we present ourselves as employees. He also lets us know that we shouldn't be slackers and not get our work done. He wants us to focus our minds and hearts on being great employees. There are different types of jobs, and we usually place judgment on one job being better than another one. God tells us in 1 Corinthians 3:7, 9, "So neither the one who plants nor the one who waters is anything, but only God, who makes things grow. For *we are co-workers in God's service;* you are God's field, God's building" (italics mine). They are differentiating in this scripture about whether one has a job planting or a job watering. God sets us straight; neither of those jobs is anything, only God. So the jobs we have are not what define us, because we are all coworkers in God's company. We are all the same because of Him. Our employer is God! He is the one who hires us to do His work, whether in the church or working at a job. God is the only one who allows us to have great impact in the world. Isaiah 42:1 states, *"Here is my servant, whom I uphold, my chosen one in whom I delight;* I will put my Spirit on him and he will *bring justice to the nations"* (italics mine). We only have the ability to make great change in the world by God choosing us to work for Him and delighting in us. It is only accomplished by God's Spirit working through us. Remember that we are God's employees. Acts 16:17 says, *"These men are the servants of the Most High God,* who are telling you the way to be saved" (italics mine). We are employees of the most high God. He has crazy, amazing plans for us! Let's petition to request that His plans will be revealed to us and that we will be led by Him. He wants us to know that we are His, that He has great plans for all of us, and that we can be hired because of Him.

Satan wants you to believe this: You have no use to God or the working world.

This is who you are: You can be hired and wanted for a valuable position by God.

Listen to Matthew West's song called "World Changers."

Do you believe that God has a specific plan for you?

Do you believe that He wants you to be able to be hired and useful?

Do you try to take control of your own life and lead the direction of your plans?

Do you present your requests about your life before God and wait for His answer?

Are you aware of the plans that God has for your life?

FIFTEEN

GOD MAKES US STABLE

We all would like a life of stability. The definition of *stable* is "able or likely to continue or last; firmly established; enduring or permanent, and having the ability to react to a disturbing force by maintaining a form" (Dictionary.com). Wouldn't we all like this to be a direct representation of our life? We want to feel stable in our lives, whether during good times or in bad. We want to have resilience, where we are able to bounce back when life hands us a raw deal. God tells us that we can be stable because He is. In Philippians 4:19, it tells us, "And *my God will meet all your* needs according to the riches of his glory in Christ Jesus" (italics mine). God is able to help us to be stable because He tells us that He will meet all our needs. He helps us when we are anxious, depressed, overwhelmed, angry, or dealing with loss, transitions, pain, and sadness. He has the ability to meet all our needs.

How does He meet all our needs and help us through difficult times? Isaiah 26:7–8 tells us how: "*The path of the righteous is level*; O upright One, you *make the way of the righteous smooth.* Yes, Lord *walking in the way of your laws, we wait for you*; your name and renown are *the desires of our hearts*" (italics mine). He actually makes the paths ahead of us level and smooth. He smooths out the road so that we will not trip or be caught up along the way. If He didn't smooth it, then there might be massive hills, very low valleys, and countless potholes. This means that the hard times in our life could be even harder if He hadn't already smoothed out the road.

Another way that God helps us through difficulties is found in Isaiah 40:28–31. "Do you not know? Have you not heard? The Lord is the everlasting God, the Creator of the ends of the earth. He will not grow tired or weary, and *His understanding no one can fathom. He gives strength to the weary and increases the power of the weak.* Even youths grow tired and weary and young men stumble and fall; but *those who hope in the Lord will renew their strength. They* will soar on wings like eagles; they will run and not grow weary, they will walk and *not grow faint*" (italics mine). When we are feeling weak and weary, He gives us strength and power. This means that we need to be leaning on His strength. I love the thought that we can soar like an eagle. He doesn't just help us gut through something hard and allow us to feel just okay. He says we will be powerful and soar and run and not grow weary! He helps us to thrive through challenging times.

What most people look for in life is love, prosperity, and the respect of others. Proverbs 21:21 tells us that very thing: "*He who pursues righteousness and love finds life, prosperity and honor*" (italics mine). If we are pursuing our own personal righteousness in our relationship with God and loving others, He promises us a pretty awesome life. He fills us up and helps us to be stable because of that. Proverbs 2:7–8 tells us, "He *holds victory in store for the upright,* He is a shield to those whose walk is blameless, for He *guards the course of the just and protects the way of His faithful one*" (italics mine). God doesn't want us not to be able to finish the race. He helps us to attain victory. He guards the course and protects our way so that we can achieve victory. Victory over addictions, compulsions, sin, and difficulties. If we are really going after being upright, He will help us to overcome these things. He is the only one who can help us to be victorious over these things and allow us the ability to find stability and balance in our life.

"The law of the Lord is perfect, *reviving the soul.* The statutes of the Lord are trustworthy, *making wise the simple.* The precepts of the Lord are right, *giving joy to the heart,* the commands of the Lord are radiant, *giving light to the eyes*" (Psalm 19:7–8; italics mine). Does this sound like a great reason to read the Bible? It says that it revives our souls. It will make my heart joyful and give light to my eyes. He revives us, makes us wise, makes us joyful, and allows us to see things clearly. This would be a definition of a stable person. We know that when we are around someone like that, we feel rejuvenated as well. This is what He offers us. How do we become like those people? Psalm 3:3 tells us, "But *you are a shield around me*, O Lord; you *bestow glory on me* and *lift up my head*" (italics mine). God builds an invisible shield around me to protect me and keep me safe from those things in the world that can tear us apart. Again, God tells us, in Psalm 54:4, "Surely *God is my help*; the Lord is *the one who sustains me*" (italics mine). Only God can help us and keep us in this fight in the world to find goodness and blessings and to be stable.

What about during really terrible and horrific times in our lives? Is God able to help me during those times when we feel like no one else could ever understand us or relate to us? At these times, we can feel all alone. Psalm 40:1–5 tells us, I waited patiently for the Lord; He turned to me and heard my cry; *He lifted me out of the slimy pit, out of the mud and mire; He set my feet on a rock and gave me a firm place to stand.* He put a new song in my mouth, a hymn of praise to our God. Many will see and fear and *put their trust in the Lord.* Blessed is the man who makes the Lord his trust, who does not look to the proud … Many, O Lord my God, are the wonders you have done. *The things you planned for us no one can recount to you*; were I to speak and tell of them, they would be too many to declare. (italics mine)

When we feel like our feet are in quicksand and that we are going to be enveloped by our fear and experiences, God tells us that He is there to lift us out of the slimy pit and He will put our feet on a firm place like a rock. We can be assured that God sees us in those dark places that we feel no one else can. And He promises us that He can help us get our footing back. He even goes on to say that He has so many things planned for success in our future that we wouldn't be able to count them they are so numerous. This is what brings us out of those dark times. Psalm 34:4–5 states, "I sought the Lord, and He answered me; *He delivered me from all my fears. Those who look to Him are radiant; their faces are never covered with shame.*" Later, in Psalm 34:18–19, it tells us, "The *Lord is close to the broken-hearted and saves those who are crushed in spirit. A righteous man may have many troubles, but the Lord delivers Him from them all*" (italics mine). God is telling us that when we feel like we are sinking and overwhelmed by fear, He cannot only deliver us from our fear but also make us radiant.

Have you ever met someone incredibly fearful? They can squash our spirits. Have you ever been around someone radiant? It lifts our spirits to be with them. This is what God promises that we can be like. He is close to the brokenhearted and crushed in spirit. You are not alone. God is close to you.

We all may go through many trials, but the Lord delivers us from them all. What type of rock does He set us on? Psalm 62:1–2 tells us, "My *soul finds rest in God alone*; my salvation comes from Him. *He alone is my rock* and my salvation; He is my fortress, *I will never be shaken*" (italics mine). We can find rest in God alone, and He is our rock and our salvation. God does not change like the passing of the guards. He is reliable, and we can stand assured on His Word and on His will for us. I really like the part that tells us that we will never be shaken.

Another scripture that tells us the same thing is in Psalm 112:4–8. It states, "*Even in darkness light dawns for the upright,* for the gracious and compassionate and righteous man. *Good will come to him* who is generous and lends freely, who conducts his affairs with justice. *Surely he will never be shaken;* a righteous man will be remembered forever. *He will have no fear of bad news; His heart is secure, he will have no fear;* in the end he will look in triumph over his foes" (italics mine). Even during the dark times, there is light. In the first five months of this year, I have lost three family members. And I don't have a big family. I have no cousins and only one uncle. But only God helps us not be shaken and for our hearts to be secure. We don't need to fear bad news. He brings stability to our life, allows us not to be shaken, and allows us to have a rock to stand on. That's how we make it through difficulties and become stable.

As a side note, if you are having mental health issues, sometimes God's way of smoothing out the road for us is with modern medicine and therapy. We can trust God that He is helping with that process if you are working with a Christian therapist who is also lifting you up in prayer to our heavenly Father. We are also given godly relationships in His kingdom that can help us to sort out our feelings and see God's plan for us.

We can have peace in our life because of what it says in Psalm 29:11: "*The Lord gives strength to His people; The Lord blesses His people with peace*" (italics mine). We don't have to live in this world with our own strength during tough times. God strengthens us and then He blesses us with peace as well. The definition of *peace* is "a state of tranquility or quiet; a state of security and order; freedom from disquieting or oppressive thoughts or emotions; or harmony in personal relations." Sounds like one of the definitions of *stable* as well. He calms our thoughts and helps us to see clearly our life situations.

A couple of years ago, my husband needed heart surgery. He was born with a bicuspid valve and it had caused an ascending aortic aneurysm. The surgery was a valve replacement and cutting out and replacing the extensive aneurysm. We were scared about the surgery and the possibility of it not going well. If I gave full reign to my thoughts, they were anxiety magnified on steroids. I went looking for a theme scripture to use as a replacement thought. My scripture was "Be still and know that I am God" (Psalm 46:10). Be still with my thoughts; be at peace because surely God had this. If He created the world, and knows us and how many hairs are on our heads, then He is just as concerned about my husband's well-being.

This is how God brings peace to our heart and thoughts. He quiets them so that He can make us stable. Psalm 119:165 says, *"Great peace have they who love your law, and nothing can make them stumble"* (italics mine). *Nothing* can make them stumble, because God gives us great peace. Wow. It's amazing how specific the scriptures are about how He cares for us and how that can completely change our lives and the direction we take. God doesn't just tell us something once. He repeats it over and over again. "You will *keep in perfect peace him whose mind is steadfast, because he trusts in You.* Trust in the Lord forever, for the Lord, the Lord, is the rock eternal" (Isaiah 26:3–4; italics mine). If we trust that God has our best interests in mind, then He promises to keep us in perfect peace. We can all have a life of peace and stability.

God is in the business of protecting, sustaining, and empowering us. He even uses heavenly beings to protect us. Psalm 91:2, 4, 11–12, tells us, "I will say of the Lord, *'He is my refuge and my fortress,* my God, in *whom I trust'*... He *will cover you with His feathers, and under his wings you will find refuge;* His faithfulness *will be your shield* and rampart. ... For He *will command His angels* concerning you *to guard you in all your ways*; *they will lift you up in their hands,* so that *you will not strike your foot against a stone"* (italics mine). He uses angels to guard us. They lift us up in their hands so that we won't get hurt. On top of that, God covers us with His feathers and protects us under his wings, just like a mother hen does her chicks. God goes to great lengths so that we can live a stable and fulfilled life. We don't have to carry the weight of the world just on our own shoulders. God wants us to understand this. *"Cast your cares on the Lord* and He *will sustain you;* He *will never let the righteous fall"* (Psalm 55:22; italics mine). He wants us to put our cares and burdens on Him. He never wants us to fall. He is willing to encourage our hearts and minds by sustaining us. Living a life of stability is all about allowing God to help us by trusting in Him and looking for His strength and direction. God wants us to be conquerors as Romans 8:37 states. "No, i*n all things we are more than conquerors through Him who loved us"* (italics mine).

Satan wants us to believe this: Our lives are unstable and we can't handle the stresses.

This is who you are: You are a stable person who can handle problems because God helps you.

Listen to Jasmine Murray's song called "Fearless."

What are situations that can cause instability?

What set of scriptures are difficult to accept as truth?

What challenging times have you been through when God has shown you His plan and sustained you?

What is the most important concept that you need to focus your learning on?

SIXTEEN

WE ARE IN THE ROYAL FAMILY

We were all born into a family. Where we were born or the family that we became a part of was not a choice we had the ability to make. Every child was created by two people, but not every child knows one or both of their parents. There are all types of families, such as two-parent homes, single-parent homes, homes with extended family, extended family members raising a child, children in orphanages, foster homes, or those adopted. Some of these families were stable, happy homes where children were loved, nourished, encouraged, mentored, and thrived. Others were raised in dysfunctional homes where they were not the focus and didn't thrive to their full potential. Our families of origin makes an impact on how we view ourselves. The problem is that this is not how God sees us. He tells us that we are children of His. We are in the family of the Creator of the universe and the Lord of all. Galatians 3:26 says, "*You are all sons of God* through faith in Christ Jesus" (italics mine). Wait. I thought that we were born into a family. But God wants us to truly understand who we are through His eyes. We are not defined by our families of origin; we are defined by our spiritual family where we have become a part of the royal family! In 2 Corinthians 6:18, it says, "'*I will be a Father* to you, and *you will be my sons and daughters*,' says the Lord" (italics mine). He tells us that we now have God as our Father and we have become His sons and daughters. This is the most amazing phenomenon.

How do we become a member of God's family? Romans 8:14–17 explains this. "For *those* who are being *led by the Spirit of God are the children of God*. The Spirit that you received does not make you slaves, so that you live in fear again; rather, the Spirit that you received *brought about your adoption to sonship*. And by him we cry, *'Abba, Father.'* The Spirit himself testifies with our spirit that *we are heirs—heirs of God and co-heirs with Christ*" (italics mine).

We enter into His family by God's Spirit who has been given to those who have chosen to live according to His will. The Spirit of God in us moves us from being slaves to becoming adopted into sonship. We go from slaves to sons and daughters. And we can approach him and call him by a very personal, intimate name of Abba or Daddy. We find this word being used by children to their fathers, whether they are small or adults. We move from being paupers and beggars to princes and princesses. Only in God's kingdom can this be true and allow it to become a reality. And what's more is that we become heirs of God and coheirs with Christ. This transformation into royalty occurs because of who God and Christ are and Their overwhelming love for us. When we become heirs, we inherit all that God and Jesus own and have to offer. This inheritance is greater than any multibillionaire family could offer or anything we could ever attain in this world.

How long has God had this plan for our adoption? Ephesians 1:4–5 gives us the answer: "For *He chose us in Him before the creation of the world* to be holy and blameless in His sight. In love, *he predestined us to be adopted as His sons through Jesus Christ*, in accordance with His pleasure and will—to the praise of His glorious grace, which He has freely given us in the One He loves" (italics mine). What? He chose us before the creation of the world, before He created humankind and even knew what we would be like as His created. He predestined us to be adopted. Meaning that He had a plan that was way before it came to be. He had this planned way before we were created! His extended plan can be found in 1 Peter 2:9–10. "But you are a *chosen people, a royal priesthood*, a holy nation, *God's special possession*, that you may declare the praises of him who called you out of darkness into his wonderful light. *Once you were not a people, but now you are the people of God*, once you had not received mercy, but now you have received mercy" (italics mine). God wants to call us out of darkness and away from not being God's people. When we heed His calling, then we become a royal priesthood, a holy nation, His special possession, and His people and receive His mercy. When we receive His mercy, He holds out His scepter as He sits on His throne of glory. And when we touch it, He doesn't just extend His mercy but says, "You are now a part of my family" and "You become royalty" as well.

Satan wants us to believe this: That we are nobody and never will be someone important; we can't change where we came from.

This is who you are: You are a part of the royal family; you are an important person and a prince or princess in God's kingdom.

Listen to Byron Cage's song "Royalty."

When looking at your family of origin, does it discolor your ability to see God's plan for your life?

What gets in your way of seeing yourself as adopted and royalty?

How would you act differently if you saw the way God looks at you as His son or daughter?

What does a person who is royalty—a prince or princess—know about themselves?

SEVENTEEN

ALL NATIONS ARE EQUAL

When we want to understand God's thoughts and feelings about equality, it is found in Psalm 99:2–4: "Great is the Lord in Zion; he is *exalted over all the nations*. Let them praise your great and awesome name-he is holy. The King is mighty, *he loves justice-you have established equity*" (italics mine). God is interested in people from all nations. The concept of justice and equality originated from Him! The definition of justice is just behavior or treatment. Synonyms of *equality* are *fairness, fair-mindedness, equity, impartiality*, and *neutrality*. The meaning of *equity* is "freedom from bias or favoritism." This is God's idea of what this world is to look like. He sees all of us as equal. We are treated without any bias or favoritism. He has instilled in each of us the gift of the Savior, salvation, the Holy Spirit, and eternity with God.

God looks at all the nations and is interested in those that love and pursue Him. Psalm 33:12–15 states, "Blessed is the *nation whose God is the Lord*, the people he *chose for his inheritance*. From heaven the *Lord looks down and sees mankind;* from his dwelling place *he watches all who live on earth—he who forms the heart of all, who considers everything they do*" (italics mine). He is seeing humankind, all the people that He has created and is interested in all that they do. He watches all who live on earth. He is not showing preferential treatment to one person over another. He calls us all to the same standard of following His truth. He has given us all the opportunity to have salvation, every one of us. Galatians 3:26–28 states, *"You are all sons of God through faith in Christ Jesus*, for *all of you* who were baptized into Christ have clothed yourselves with Christ. There is *neither Jew nor Greek, slave nor free, male nor female, for you are all one in Christ"* (italics mine). I love the statement that we are all one in Christ. Whether we are red, black, yellow, or white, we are equal and one in Christ. This is the epitome of equality!

We are all sons and daughters of God, through our faith in Him. The world is made up of 196 nations. That means that every one of them is equal in God's eyes. The world may have its own opinions and slants toward different nationalities, but the truth is that God created us equal. Psalm 24:1–4 tells us, *"The earth is the Lord's and everything in it, the world and all who live in it*; for He founded it upon the seas and established it upon the waters. Who may ascend the hill of the Lord? *Who may stand in His holy place? He who has clean hands and a pure heart.* Who does not lift up his soul to an idol or swear by what is false" (italics mine). God created everything and everyone. How can we stand in His holy place? Anyone who is willing to pursue holiness and deal with the sin in their lives. Everyone is held to the same standard in God. He again is discussing the topic of equality. We are all equal before God. Our relationship with Him is the great equalizer and unifier. This was God's plan to have all people unified before Him.

Being a part of His kingdom on earth is our greatest blessing to be able to have relationships with every nationality. We should never take this blessing for granted. Deuteronomy 7:6 helps us to understand that. "For *you are a people holy to the Lord* your God. The Lord your God *has chosen you out of all the peoples on the face of the earth to be his people, His treasured possession"* (italics mine). We have all had the incredible chance to be chosen out of this world to be His treasured possession. What should we do with this great gift of salvation and equality in God's kingdom? Revelation 7:9–10 states, "After this I looked, and there before me was a *great multitude* that no one could count, *from every nation, tribe, people and language, standing before the throne* and before the Lamb. They were wearing white robes and were holding palm branches in their hands. And they cried out in a loud voice: salvation belongs to our God, who sits on the throne, and to the Lamb" (italics mine). Each nation, tribe, people, and language is all-encompassing. All of us were praising God together and worshipping our great and awesome God.

Isn't this the kind of message that you want to share with others? Mark 16:15 tells us, "He said to them, *'Go into all the world and preach the gospel among all nation'*" (italics mine). Our mission is to share with the whole world and every nation His incredible blessings that He gives us. We get to be equal to one another and experience all the blessings that come with that. "May God be *gracious to us* and *bless us* and make His face shine on us—so that *your ways may be known on earth, your salvation among all nations*" (Psalm 67:1–2; italics mine). Let's be grateful for God saving all people and treating all of us equally and then turn around and share it with others.

Satan wants us to believe this: Some races are more important than others and this will never change.

This is who you are: You are equal to every other nationality, color, or ethnicity.

Listen to the Mandisa song "Bleed the Same."

Do you ever feel that your nationality makes you less or greater than others?

What type of freedom does God want us to experience in His kingdom?

What is most challenging about this concept?

What kind of lies has Satan been telling you?

EIGHTEEN

WE HAVE HOPE

We live in a world where hopelessness is common and hopeful people are not. Whether it's the forecast of our nation or your life situation, there are way too many stressors that can make our lives feel dark and hopeless. I have worked with many whose world was bleak and who had limited hope. Health issues, family or marital conflict, addictions, depression, anxiety, domestic violence, inability to have children, losses either from death, jobs, housing, or life transitions can cause people to wonder about their life and what the future holds. God gives us the answer for hopelessness. Jeremiah 29:11 gives us His perspective. "'For I know the *plans* I have *for you*', declares the Lord, '*plans to prosper* you and not to harm you, plans to *give you hope and a future*'" (italics mine). He knows exactly what our lives will be filled with and what our future holds. God wants us to understand that His will for us is that we prosper and can have hope and a future. This is the answer for the hopelessness of the world.

We can have hope because of the plans that He knows and has for us. Proverbs 23:18 is another reminder of our future. "There is *surely a future hope for you, and your hope will not be cut off*" (italics mine). We are promised hope in our future and are reminded that this type of hope cannot be cut off. This means that hope has no end. Is there a limit to your hope? Is this kind of hope for just the young or for those older? Psalm 71:5 says, "For *you have been my hope*, O Sovereign Lord, *my confidence since my youth*" (italics mine). Our Lord states that this hope is from young on up. There is no start or end age that God does not fill us up with hope. Is this the kind of life that you'd like to live? One filled to the brim with hope for the future?

I know that there are cynics who think that it's just too simplistic to have hope filling your life. Maybe you relate more with the scripture found in Psalm 43:5. "*Why, my soul, are you downcast? Why so disturbed* within me? *Put your hope in God*, for I will yet praise Him, my Savior and my God*" (italics mine). We all relate with the dark times where we feel sad and at unrest internally and don't see or feel hope. This scripture says that we need to put our hope in God. This is an action word that requires us to put it into practice. If we understand that God is the giver of hope, then we have a bank of hope ready for us to tap into. We need only to take it. Maybe you need to picture a real bank. If you are feeling defeated, then you go to the bank and request a large withdrawal. Or if you only feel you need a hope boost, then withdraw a smaller amount from the Bank of Hope. Either way, we have hope at our disposal. We need only make a request of God. Romans 12:12 also tells us what to do when we are low in hope. "*Be joyful in hope, patient in affliction, faithful in prayer*" (italics mine). Hope makes us feel joyful, and even through affliction we can devote ourselves to prayer. We can ask our heavenly Father to fill us to the brim with hope. I want a full cup. Look at Lamentations 3:21–23. "Yet this I call to mind and therefore I *have hope*: Because of the *Lord's great love* we are not consumed, his *compassions never fail*. They are new every morning; great is your faithfulness" (italics mine). Sometimes we can feel consumed by grief, just like in the definition of *lament,* which is a passionate expression of grief. We have the hope of God's faithfulness every morning. We get a chance to start over every day, because of the Lord's great love and compassion for us. These are the concepts that we gain hope from.

One of the most amazing ways that can develop our hope is to truly understand the great gift that we have received in our salvation. We can, at times, forget where we came from before we were considered children of God. These scriptures will be a great reminder of what we have received and the hope that it produces. In 1 Peter 1:18–21, it states, "For you know that it was not with perishable things such as silver or gold that you were *redeemed from the empty way of* life handed down to you from your ancestors, but *with the precious blood of Christ*, a lamb without blemish or defect. He was chosen before the creation of the world, but was revealed in these last times for your sake. *Through him you believe in God.* Who raised Him from the dead and glorified him, and *so your faith and hope are in God*" (italics mine). We were living an empty way of life, filled with so many sins that stole our hope. We have been redeemed by Jesus's perfect sacrifice on the cross. His sacrifice allowed us to have a relationship with God and allows us to have faith and hope in God. We are only allowed to have hope because of our salvation given to us by Christ. Our salvation has also saved us from much heartache and pain. Only through this can we have the blessing of hope.

We not only have the hope of salvation, but we also have the riches of inheritance in the life to come. It tells us in Ephesians 1:18, "I pray that the *eyes of your heart may* be enlightened in order *that you may know the hope to which he has called you, the riches of his glorious inheritance in his holy people*" (italics mine). We lose sight of what brings us hope: His calling to us about His glorious inheritance for us. Our eyes need enlightened. We might need glasses, contacts, or surgery to see the hope that He has called us to. Sometimes we can be focusing and looking at the wrong things. Those wrong things are the very ways that keep us feeling hopeless. We need to focus on remembering the very hope of salvation and the inheritance given us. These are the concepts that brought us hope in the past. Again, it speaks of our inheritance in Titus 3:7. "So that, having been *justified by His grace*, we might *become heirs having the hope of eternal life*" (italics mine). We have the hope of eternal life! We also remain hopeful by our gratitude for God's grace.

We can have hope that we will not have to pay for what our sins deserve. First Peter 1:3 speaks about his grace and mercy. "Praise be to the God and Father of our Lord Jesus Christ! In *His great mercy* he has *given us new birth into a living hope* through the resurrection of Jesus Christ from the dead" (italics mine). Because of Christ's great mercy, we are given new birth into a living hope. This means that it can be renewed every morning. Hope is not dead but alive in us. We only can gain hope when we understand, are grateful, and focus on our salvation and the grace we have been given.

What happens to our hope when we go through trials and hardships?

James 1:12 tells us the answer to this question. *"Blessed is the man who perseveres under trial,* because when he has stood the test, he will *receive the crown of life* that God has promised to those that love Him" (italics mine). We are blessed when we go through hardship? Maybe Romans 5:3–5 explains it in a clearer manner. "Not only so, but we also *rejoice in our sufferings,* because we know that suffering, *produces perseverance;* perseverance, *character;* and character, *hope.* And *hope* does not disappoint us, because God has poured out his love into our hearts by the Holy Spirit *whom He has given us"* (italics mine).

God has a plan for good things to come even through hardships. He is always working to mold and shape us into the people He can use for greater purposes. Trials and hardship produce in us perseverance, character, and then hope. Hope will not disappoint us because God pours His love into us. We can't gain hope without all the inner workings in our hearts that God has ordained to His beauty to be revealed in us. Not only do we gain inner qualities, but Job 11:18 tells us that we will be secure as well. "You will *be secure, because there is hope;* you will look about you and take your *rest in safety"* (italics mine). When we endure difficult times, hope allows us to feel secure and we will be able to look around us and know that we can rest safely in his safety. We are firmly planted in God's hope. Hebrews 6:19 says, "We *have this hope as an anchor for the soul, firm and secure"* (italics mine). Anchors are used to keep a ship from drifting by the winds or the wave. They are dropped into the ocean and the ship becomes immovable by anything. This scripture describes what hope is for us: firm and secure. You can be assured that God wants us to rely on Him. He creates character development and security.

There are endless scriptures on the topic of hope. Why? Because God wants you to know that you can live a life full of hope. We can be filled to the top of our hearts with hope when we are close to God, remember the gift of salvation, and keep from focusing on the wrong thoughts. I love the simplicity of Psalm 39:7. "But now, Lord, *what do I look for? My hope is in you"* (italics mine). We need the reminder to be looking for hope. Some of us have become too comfortable with being pessimists and only focusing on problems. What we need to be focusing on is God and His promises. As a doxology and ending thought, I leave you with Romans 15:13. "May the *God of hope fill you with all joy and peace as you trust in Him*, so that you *may overflow with hope by the power of the Holy Spirit*" (italics mine).

Satan wants us to believe this: There is no hope in the world and nothing to hope for.

This is who you are: A hopeful person because God offers hope for the future.

Listen to the Tauren Well song "Hills and Valleys."

What thoughts do you get stuck on that get you offtrack?

Is living a life filled with hope something you have a hard time imagining?

What type of life does God want for you with hope?

Which scripture or scriptures encourage you the most? Why not memorize them?

NINETEEN

WE ARE IMPORTANT ENOUGH TO GET TOP-SECRET INTEL

The title of this chapter may have you wondering what in the world this chapter is about. We are the children of God, created by Him and for Him. As such, we are privy to important information that others are not aware of. First Corinthians 4:1–2 is the theme scripture and tells us, "This, then, is how you ought to regard us: as *servants of Christ* and as those *entrusted with The secret things of God*. Now it is *required* that those who have been *given a trust* must *prove faithful*" (italics mine).

We have been entrusted with the very mysteries of God that He has revealed to us. That makes us important enough to have top-secret information divulged to us. This has only been given to those who are servants of the living God. It allows us to be able to understand hidden meanings behind the story, like parables. Psalm 78:2 explains this phenomenon. "I will open my mouth with a parable; I will *utter hidden things, things from of old*" (italics mine). A parable is a story that casts alongside a truth in order to illustrate that truth. Jesus used parables to tell an earthly story with a heavenly meaning. Not everyone who heard the parable understood the underlying meaning. The disciples were given the inside meaning, as we who are believers do as well. In John 15:15, Jesus says, "I no longer call you servants, because a servant does not know his master's business. Instead, I have called you friends, for everything that I learned from my Father I have made known to you." We are friends and close to the affairs of the Lord. Because of this, we know our Master's business. He keeps us in the loop and has given us so much inside information just in His Word alone that we have readily available to us. He gives us the opportunity to have the inside scoop from His Word and then allows His Spirit to help us to deeply understand His glorious plan.

Some have been blinded to the truth because of their lack of desire to be molded to God's plan for their lives. For those whose desire is to know God, it tells us in Psalm 25:14, "The Lord confides in those who fear Him; He makes His covenant known to them." When we understand that He is the ruler of all and we are not, it causes us to have a deep reverence of Him. When we comprehend the ordering of the relationship, He confides in us.

What information does He confide to us? Maybe He confides the intimate story of His salvation, His great plans for us, the missions for our lives, or His unending love, concern, and grace. "The *secret things belong to the Lord* our God, but *the things revealed belong to us and to our children forever*, that we may follow all the words of this law" (Deuteronomy 29:29; italics mine).

God reveals secrets to not only us but to our children as well. Why does He reveal these secrets? So that we can follow all the words of His law. We get the opportunity to hear the very words of God in the Bible. In His Word, He shows us His secrets and His plan of how to understand who He is and how to be close to Him. He gives us the plan of how to be our best as humans. These are His secrets for us to be able to function best.

Another scripture that helps us see what God wants us to understand is Daniel 2:22. "He *reveals deep and hidden things*; he *knows what lies in darkness* and *light dwells with him*" (italics mine). God reveals deep and hidden things. Revealing deep and hidden things measures the intimate details of what He is giving to us. If He knows what hides in the darkness, then we do too. Light symbolizes God, and darkness represents everything that is not of God. Although in the dark we cannot see what we are doing that is wrong, it is transparent to God. Only through salvation do we move from darkness into light.

On the internet, I found a list of 667 sins pointed out in specifics and in generalities. Some specific sins on that list are murder, gossip, pride, arrogance, lust, greed, taking God's name in vain, jealousy, fits of rage, witchcraft, foul language, stealing, love of money, easily angered, worshipping idols, selfish ambition, the love of money, overindulging, lack of forgiveness, lying, adultery, and causing someone else to sin. When we seek God and come into His light, He reveals the hidden things that are a part of the light. We get the great gift of having our eyes opened by God's truth and then can see clearly all the things in our lives that are a part of the darkness. Amos 3:7 informs us, "Surely the Sovereign Lord does nothing without revealing His plan to his servants the prophets." That is the type of God that we serve who does nothing without revealing His plan to us. That is so amazing that we get inside information revealed to us.

Not only do we understand what is in the light, but we also receive inside information from God's Spirit and for those in God's church. 1 Corinthians 2:9–10, 12, reveals to us, "*No eye* has seen, *no ear* has heard, *no mind has conceived what God has prepared for those who love Him*'… but *God has revealed it to us by His Spirit*. The Spirit *searches all things, even the deep things of God*. We have not *received* the spirit of the world but the *spirit who is from God, that we may understand what God has freely given us*." First Corinthians 2:10b, 16b states, "The *Spirit searches all things, even the deep things of God. … But we have the mind of Christ*" (italics mine). Because we have God's Spirit, we can see, hear, and understand what God has revealed to us. The Spirit searches all thing, even the deep things, and we can comprehend on a deep level because we have the mind of God. We have been given a part of God in us through the Spirit. So we can understand the deep revelations of God in a way that nonbelievers cannot comprehend.

He tells us that the Spirit helps us understand what God has freely given us. Romans 8:27 speaks of the Spirit's role in our lives as well. "And *He who searches the hearts knows the mind of the Spirit,* because the *Spirit intercedes for God's people in accordance with the will of God*" (italics mine). God knows us and the Spirit is the go-between for us with God and how we learn to act in step with God's will. We can be assured that God intercedes for His people through His Spirit that we have freely been given. In Ephesians 3:4–6, it says, "*You will be able to understand my insight into the mystery of Christ*, which was not made known to people in other generations as it *has now been revealed by the Spirit to God's holy apostles and prophets. This mystery is that through the gospel the Gentiles are heirs together in the promise in Christ Jesus"* (italics mine). This scripture explains that we will be able to understand His insight about the mystery of Christ.

There were many who did not accept or perceive that Jesus was the Christ and the Son of the Holy God. This was a mystery that God would send down His own Son in human form and allow Him to be raised in humble circumstances. To live in all the imperfections of humanness and experience all the hardships that He did. These truths have been revealed to us. Through the gospel, we have the opportunity to be heirs in the promise of Jesus. This in an amazing concept. It then goes on in Ephesians 3:9–12. "And *to make plain to everyone the administration of this mystery, which for ages past was kept hidden in God;* who created all things. *His intent was that now through the church, the manifold wisdom of God should be known* to the rulers and authorities in the heavenly realms, according to his eternal purpose which He accomplished in Christ Jesus our Lord. *In Him and through faith in Him we may approach God with freedom and confidence"* (italics mine). It has been made plain to everyone the mystery that in ages past was hidden. But now His intent is that the church should have the manifold wisdom of God. Because of this great information, we can now approach God with freedom and confidence. Wow. The church has been instilled with a great mystery about God, and He lets us come directly to Him unabashedly.

We have been blessed with amazing information and wisdom. Since we can come freely to God with freedom and confidence, He also tells us that He hears us when we approach Him. Psalm 4:3 states, "Know that *the Lord has set apart the godly for Himself;* the Lord *will hear when I call to Him"* (italics mine). We have a direct line to God and His ear. He also states that the Lord has set us apart for Him. He hears when I call to Him, because He knows the voice of His own children. For those of you who have children, when they speak, you know their voices and are fully interested in what they want to tell you. This is the same manner that God feels about us. Psalm 5:3 states, *"In the morning, O Lord, you hear my voice;* in the morning I *lay my requests before you and wait in expectation"* (italics mine). We can request important things to the King of heaven and earth and wait for Him to answer, because He does answer us. We get to hear from the Big Boss!

Isaiah 65:24 explains that God knows what we will say before we do. *"Before they call I will answer; while they are still speaking I will hear"* (italics mine). We have a Lord who knows us so well that He knows what we will pray and is already answering and hearing us. God wants to grant our requests. In John 15:7, it tells us, "If you *remain in me* and my words remain in you, *ask whatever you wish and it will be given* to you" (italics mine). We need to understand on a deep level that we need to remain close to God and His words. When we do, He wants to bless us and says that all we need to do is to ask whatever we wish and He will give it to us. We have the most amazing boss of all. He instills us with knowledge about His mysteries and blesses us with His Spirit and the church and always hears us when we call.

Satan wants us to believe this: We will never be important enough or smart enough to be a part of inside information entrusted by God.

This is who you are: You are an important person who God invests secrets to and who listens to your thoughts.

Listen to the Jason Gray song called "Sparrows."

Have you ever thought about God revealing His mysteries to us?

Why does He speak clearly to us with His deep knowledge?

Now understanding the mysteries revealed to us, how does that change how you feel about yourself?

What type of communication are you having with God as He hears you and wants to answer your request?

TWENTY

OUR MISTAKES ARE FORGOTTEN

W e are not defined by our mistakes but by our successes, growth, and the little ways that we make a difference in others' lives. We have been blessed to be able to worship a God who does not treat us as our sins deserve. It's difficult for us to comprehend grace, mercy, and forgiveness. The theme scripture is found in Psalm 86:5, 8–10, which says, "*You are forgiving and good, O Lord, abounding in love for all who call to you. … Among the gods there is none like you*, O Lord; no deeds can compare with yours. *All the nations you have made will come and worship before you*, O Lord; they will bring glory to your name. *For you are great* and do marvelous deeds; *you alone are God*" (italics mine). There is no other God than our God. This is whom we worship and whom we should glorify. He is a forgiving God and good, abounding in love for all who call on Him. We should call Him marvelous and great. We are so blessed that we get the opportunity to have our sins wiped clean. "But you, O Lord, are a *compassionate and gracious God, slow to anger, abounding in love* and *faithfulness*. Turn to me and *have mercy on me*" (Psalm 86:15–16; italics mine). We are shown compassion, grace, slow anger, abounding love, faithfulness, and mercy. Wow!

We need to realize that the mistakes we've made in the past and our current sins are forgiven. What type of punishment do we deserve for our sins? We deserve death and punishment for them. And yet Psalm 103:2–5 tells us, *"Praise the Lord, my soul, and forget not all his benefits*-who *forgives all your sins* and heals all your diseases, who redeems your life from the pit and crowns you with love and *compassion, who satisfies your desires with good things* so that your youth is renewed like the eagle's." Verses 9–10 say, *"He will not always accuse* nor will he harbor his anger forever; he *does not treat us as our sins deserve or repay us according to our iniquities"* (italics mine). We should not forget the benefits of a relationship with God. He forgives our sins, heals all our diseases, redeems our lives from the pit, and then puts a crown on our heads of love and compassion. On top of that, He satisfies our desires with good things. He does not treat us as our sins deserve or pay us with the consequences of our iniquities. This is why we need to remember all the gifts from God, because it keeps us grateful and centered.

Another reason that we need to keep it at the forefront of our minds is to help keep us humble and in pursuit of righteousness and holiness. This process is explained in 2 Chronicles 7:14. "If my people, who are called by my name, will *humble themselves and pray and seek my face and turn from their wicked ways,* then will I hear from heaven and *will forgive their sin* and *will heal their land"* (italics mine). Our part of the process is to stay humble when we sin and turn away from it. We need to pray for forgiveness and seek God's face and not turn away from Him in shame from our misdeeds. If we seek Him, He says that He will forgive our sins and heal us. Being forgiven is not something we earn; it is simply a gift that we do not deserve. Yet He chooses to offer this gift freely if we follow Him. Psalm 32:1–2, 4–5, states, *"Blessed is he whose transgressions are forgiven, whose sins are covered.* Blessed is the man *whose sin the Lord does not count against him* … For day and night your hand was heavy upon me; my strength was sapped as in the heat of summer. *Then I acknowledged my sin* and did not cover up my iniquity. I said, '*I will confess my transgressions to the Lord'-you forgave the guilt of my sin"* (italics mine).

We cannot thrive when we are steeped in sin. We feel the weight of God's hand until we are willing to acknowledge our own sin and confess them to the Lord. Then He forgives the guilt of our sin. We then become blessed because our transgressions are forgiven and our sins are buried and covered over. God only wants us to thrive by being aware of our sins and to avoid committing them. Psalm 119:133 explains the reason why. *"Direct my footsteps according to your word; let no sin rule over me"* (italics mine). If we give full reign to a sin, it can literally rule our lives and all the consequences that come with it. Take alcohol for instance. If used in moderation, it is not necessarily bad. If you have no limits on how much alcohol you consume, it can become addictive and rule your life and your choices. You begin basing your schedule around alcohol and consuming it, as well as the amount of money spent on it and the negative impact on yourself and others. Psalm 78:38 states, "Yet *he was merciful; he forgave their iniquities* and did not destroy them. *Time after time he restrained his anger* and did not stir up his full wrath" (italics mine). We are given ample opportunity to repent and turn from our ways, because of His mercifulness, restrained anger, and consistent forgiveness. And He doesn't keep our sin in His back pocket to pull out to remind us of our faults. Instead, He says, "*As far as the east is from the west, so far has he removed our transgressions from us*" (Psalm 103:12; italics mine). No, He takes our sin and removes it to the polar extremes. As far as the east is from the west, He removes our sin. That means that He is not sitting around thinking about all our faults and past sins. He casts them far away. When we understand that God does not look at us as faulty, we can feel free and good about ourselves.

God loves us immensely, and because He does, He tells us in Nehemiah 9:17, "But *you* are a forgiving God, gracious and compassionate, slow to anger and abounding in love." Because God loves us so much, He wants us to understand how He views us. He wants us to feel forgiven and loved. What could influence our self-esteem more than that? He loved us so much that He was willing to allow Jesus to be the sacrifice to cover over our sin. Second Corinthians 5:21 tells us, "*God made Him who had no sin to be sin for us, so that in Him we might become the righteousness of God*" (italics mine). Through Jesus's sacrifice, we become the righteousness of God! The impact of this thought should make us thoroughly cherish who we are in Christ.

Satan wants us to believe this: Our mistakes can never be erased and everyone, including God, will look at us as a series of mistakes.

This is who you are: One whose mistakes are forgotten and sins forgiven.

Listen to Tenth Avenue North's song "You Are More."
Listen to the Casting Crowns' song "East to West."
Listen to the Sidewalk Prophets' song "You Love Me Anyway."

What is the hardest part to accept about our sins being forgiven and forgotten?

Why does God choose to forgive us?

Are there any sins that you don't feel God can forgive?

How should you feel about yourself, knowing that God chooses to forgive you?

TWENTY-ONE

WE ARE RICH

Whether we are rich or poor in the world's eyes, we are always rich because of God. Second Corinthians 8:9 tells us, "For you know *the grace of our Lord Jesus Christ, that though He was rich, yet for your sakes He became poor, so that you through His poverty might become rich*" (italics mine). Wow. He was willing to become poor so that we could be rich! This is like a millionaire deciding to give all his millions to a pauper on the streets. That person who was made rich happened because the millionaire was willing to become poor. The pauper didn't earn the ability to becoming rich; it was an undeserved gift. So Jesus makes us rich because He wants us to feel rich. It is not by anything we did that makes us worthy. It is merely a gift. Psalm 119:14 states, "*I rejoice in following your statutes as one rejoices in great riches*" (italics mine).

One way that we are rich is because of our chance to know God's will from His words in the scriptures. Ephesians 2:6–7 says, "And *God raised us up with Christ and seated us with Him in the heavenly realms* in Christ Jesus, in order that in the coming ages *He might show the incomparable riches of His grace, expressed in His kindness to us* in Christ Jesus" (italics mine). We receive riches by God being gracious to us because of Christ's sacrifice for us. We have the gift of being raised up with Christ in heaven. It also says in Colossians 1:27, "To them *God has chosen to make known* among the Gentiles the *glorious riches* of this mystery, which is *Christ in you, the hope of glory*" (italics mine). God chose to let us know about the glorious riches we receive from Christ. He gives us hope to be glorified with Him. So we are rich by knowing His Word and by His kindness and grace given to us.

Should we chase after working to be being rich in this life? Proverbs 23:4–5 says to us, "*Do not wear yourself out to get rich; have the wisdom to show restraint. Cast but a glance at riches, and they are gone,* for they will surely sprout wings and fly off to the sky like an eagle" (italics mine). Worldly riches are fleeting, and we are not guaranteed that they will last. We cannot put our hope in that which will not last. We need unshakeable riches. Those riches only God can offer us. Jeremiah 9:23–24 tells us, "This is what the Lord says, '*Let not* the wise man boast of his wisdom, or the strong man boast of his strength or *the rich man boast of his riches,* but let him who boasts boast about this: that he understands and knows me, that I am the Lord, who exercises kindness, *justice and righteousness on earth, for in these I delight,*' declares the Lord" (italics mine). This indicates that being truly rich is not those who are financially rich but those who know and understand our Lord and who act like Him with kindness, justice, and righteousness. God delights in these things. Our financial richness is not what is important to God but our richness in Christ. Matthew 19:23–24 says, "Then Jesus said to His disciples, 'I tell you the truth, *it is hard for a rich man to enter the kingdom of heaven.* Again, I tell you, it is *easier for a camel to go through the eye of a needle than for a rich man to enter the kingdom of God*'" (italics mine). So money does not make us rich. Money is a distraction from what really makes us rich—God and knowing Him!

What should we be focusing on? In Proverbs 30:8–9, it tells us, "Keep falsehood and lies far from me; *give me neither poverty nor riches, but give me only my daily bread.* Otherwise, I *may have too much and disown you* and say, 'Who is the Lord?' Or I *may become poor and steal and so dishonor the name of my God*" (italics mine). In worldly riches, it is better not be too poor or too rich but to learn to be grateful for what God has blessed us with and to learn the gift of contentment. First Timothy 6:6–10 explains this concept. "But *godliness with contentment is great gain. For we brought nothing into the world and we can take nothing out of it.* But *if we have food and clothing, we will be content with that.* People who want to get rich fall into temptation and a trap and into many foolish and harmful desires that plunge men into ruin and destruction. For *the love of money is a root of all kinds of evil*. Some people eager for money have *wandered from the faith and pierced themselves with many griefs*." It says in verse 17, "*Command those who are rich in this present world not to be arrogant nor to put their hope in wealth*, which is so uncertain, but to *put their hope in God, who richly provides us with everything for our enjoyment*" (italics mine). God wants us to feel rich in Him and to learn to be content with whatever we have been given financially. Money can lead us into sin when we pursue it and desire more. We shouldn't be worried about reveling in our wealth but to put our hope in God, who richly provides us with everything for our enjoyment. This is worthy of repeating. He gives us everything for our enjoyment.

When looking at all Paul's hardships, it tells us in 2 Corinthians 6:10, "Poor, yet making many rich, *having nothing, yet possessing everything*" (italics mine). Everything refers to the others that Paul made rich by his preaching, even though he was poor. God offers to take care of all our needs and more.

Many wealthy people are not happy in life, content, or full of depth of character or knowledge of God. There are examples of those who are very rich having very unhealthy lifestyles and chasing after happiness, only to find that it doesn't make them happy. Ecclesiastes 2:26 states, "*To the person who pleases him, God gives wisdom, knowledge and happiness*, but *to the sinner he gives the task of gathering and storing up wealth to hand it over to the one who pleases God*" (italics mine). This is the way of the rich, focused on the task of gathering and storing up wealth. The problem is that their wealth will be given over to the one who pleases God. God gives us the greater wealth of wisdom, knowledge, and happiness. We receive these greater gifts from God and not from chasing after worldly wealth. Matthew 6:19–21 reminds us of this. "*Do not store up for yourselves treasures on earth*, where moth and rust destroy, and where thieves break in a steal. But *store up for yourselves treasures in heaven*, where moth and rust do not destroy, and where thieves do not break in and steal. For *where your treasure is, there your heart will be also*" (italics mine).

In order to store up something, whether it be crops, money, or collectives, it takes time and attention. You can't store up something without focusing on it. The problem with things is that they can wear out and get ruined or even be stolen. When we store up things focused on heavenly possessions, then those are treasures that cannot be ruined. What we focus our attention and time on is how we show where our hearts really are. Ephesians 1:18–19 says, "I pray that the *eyes of your heart may be enlightened* in order that you may *know the hope* to which He has called you, the *riches of his glorious inheritance in the saints*, and his *incomparably great power for us who believe*. That power is like the working of his mighty strength" (italics mine). We need our heart enlightened so that we can see how rich we will be having a future glorious inheritance. He gives us incomparably great power! "Listen my dear brothers: Has not God chosen those who are poor in the eyes of the world to be rich in faith and to inherit the *kingdom* He promised those who love Him?" (James 2:5; italics mine). We are millionaires, or even billionaires, because of the richness that God has given us who believe.

Satan wants us to believe this: We will never be rich in anything; we will be poor in money and spirit.

This is who you are: You are rich; you have the things that everyone is looking for in this world plus treasures in heaven.

Listen to the song by Manic Drive called "Money."

What worldly possessions are you temped to place a lot of importance on?

Does the world tempt you into thinking that the pursuit of wealth and becoming rich is really important and praiseworthy?

How does God make you rich, and in what ways?

What concept of the richness of God do you have difficulty believing or accepting?

GOD'S INFLUENCE ON SELF-ESTEEM

Identify your own

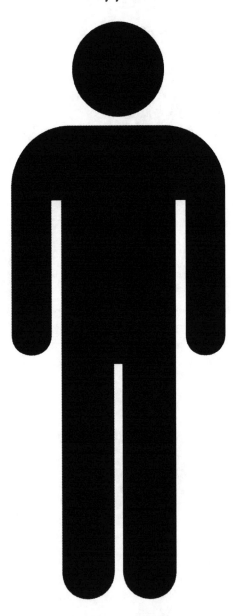

—————— PART 3 ——————

WHAT HEALTHY SELF-ESTEEM LOOKS LIKE

TWENTY-TWO

THINKING ABOUT
THE POSITIVE

Would you consider yourself a pessimist or an optimist? Pessimists are focused on what they do not have or what is wrong in their world. They are always looking to make changes but feel that the stark reality of life is faulty. Maybe you've heard the pessimist statement "It's always something" or "If it's not one thing, it's another." Yes, we can admit that there are many negative things in our world that if focused on could occupy our head space with extreme negativity. Optimists know that the reality of life can be negative but still choose to look on the positive side, even of a negative event. There are two sides to every situation, and we all have a choice of how we look at it. I'm all for dealing with reality, but there are blessings in our lives every day, and an optimist is the ones who looks for those blessings and fills their mind with them.

Let's take a look at what the scriptures tell us we should fill our minds with. In Philemon 4:8, it tells us, "Finally, brothers, *whatever is true*, whatever is *noble*, whatever is *right*, whatever is *pure*, whatever is *lovely*, whatever is *admirable*-if anything is *excellent* or *praiseworthy-think about such things*" (italics mine). Wow. The scripture tells us so clearly that we should fill our hearts and minds with positive and optimistic thoughts. How do we change our thoughts to positive ones? God tells us that we need to become and think like Him. In Isaiah 55:8, God tells us why we need to be close to Him. "For *my thoughts are not your thoughts, neither are your ways my ways*" (italics mine).

Think about what happens when we give our minds full reign to focus on the worst-case scenario. Our thoughts can become dark very quickly. It only starts with one negative thought, and before you realize it, your thinking spirals down. I use the example of these dark thoughts being like flushing a toilet. The thoughts spiral down in a whirlwind of negativity, and the result is ending up in the dark sewer. Many wonder how they got to that dark place. It is hard to get back from that dark place, because you're not sure how you even got there. It all started by filling your mind with negative, pessimistic, or even fatalistic thoughts. This is why it's so important to look at the bright side of our life situations. Another life example is looking at a rosebush. What does a rosebush look like? For those cutting back a rosebush, it is full of very sharp thorns. To those looking at a rosebush, there are beautiful flowers. Which perception is right? Both are, but we should be more apt to adore the beauty of the flower that God gave us for our enjoyment than the thorns that can puncture our hands and make them bleed. Hebrews 12:2 reminds us of our only hope to having positive thoughts. "Let us *fix our eyes on Jesus*, the author and perfecter of our faith" (italics mine).

At the end of my counseling sessions, I always give my clients a positive statement fortune from my bowl of self-esteem. Although many of these fortunes are secular, they still focus us on the positive. I decided to make a list below of some positive statements from my bowl. These are positive thoughts that you could read through daily to fill your mind with positivity, optimism, and hope.

- Having a positive mental attitude is asking how something can be done rather than saying it can't be done. (Bo Bennett)
- Optimism is a self-fulfilling prophecy. (Jeanette Walls)
- Attitude is 90% and circumstances is 10.
- Joy is not a matter of what's happening around you, but inside you. (Steve Miller)
- This is our predicament: Over and over again, we lose sight of what is important and what is not. (Epictetus)
- The happiness of your life depends on the quality of your thoughts. (Marcus Aurelius)

- A positive attitude causes a chain reaction of positive thoughts, events, and outcomes. It is a catalyst and it sparks extraordinary results. (Wade Boggs)
- Your attitude is an expression of your values, beliefs, and expectations. (Brian Tracy)
- Your attitude is like a box of crayons that color your world. Constantly color your picture gray, and your picture will always be bleak. Try adding some bright colors to the picture by including humor, and your picture begins to lighten up. (Allen Klein)
- The mind is everything. What you think you become. (Buddha)

Does reading over these positive thoughts help you understand how important these types of thoughts are to your self-esteem? There are negative thoughts swirling all around us in the media, in the news, from others, and from ourselves. We can be the worst culprit of negative self-talk. We often tell ourselves all kinds of negative thoughts about ourselves and our world that are not based on truth. If the choice is not to think positively, then what is the other alternative? It is to be critical and negative.

For those of us who have a hard time staying positive, we have a Spirit that can help us. In Romans 8:27, it says, "And *he who searches our hearts knows the mind of the Spirit*, because the *Spirit intercedes* for God's people in accordance with the will of God" (italics mine). We can be helped by God's Spirit to keep our minds positive. Psalm 27:13 shows us what we should be looking for in the world. It says, "I remain confident of this: *I will see the goodness of the Lord in the land* of the living" (italics mine). What if we looked for the goodness of the Lord in our lives? It's like watching the news on TV, the difference that we see and feel between the negative stories and those that are inspiring and positive. Psalm 118:24 says, "The Lord has done it this very day; *let us rejoice today and be glad*" (italics mine).

We need to fill our minds with positive thoughts. I suggest finding a replacement thought for when the negative thoughts come to mind. The best way to do that is to find a theme scripture for those times. Use this technique to remind us what we should be focused on in God. A healthy self-esteem is when someone fills their thoughts and mind on the positive and is willing to fight to keep it that way.

Listen to "Counting Every Blessing" by Rend Collectives.

Would you consider yourself an optimist or a pessimist?

Are there areas of your life that you find harder to keep positive thoughts in?

Do you have negative self-talk, and if so, what do you say?

What is a good replacement thought or scripture that would help you in negative thoughts and times?

TWENTY-THREE

ACCEPT THAT YOU HAVE STRENGTHS AND WEAKNESSES

Most of us are able to identify our negative traits more quickly than our positive ones. I use an exercise and homework assignment with my clients. They write a list of the things that they like about themselves. I let them know that I want at least fifteen on that list. The positive things can be strengths in character or in relationships, body characteristics, hobbies, things about their jobs, and so on. I can't tell you how many times clients are not able to find even ten things they like about themselves. But ask them to come up with a list of things that they don't like about themselves, and they have no problem making a long list. The only problem they find with the homework assignment is that the list of things that they don't like about themselves cannot be as long as the list of the things that they like. I often have to ask leading questions to help them elongate the list of the things that they like about themselves.

The truth is that there are both good and bad characteristics in all of us. On this side of eternity, there are no perfect people. Can we accept that in each of us are positive and negative parts at the same time? At times, we find that a negative characteristic or "problem" part of us can overshadow everything else. We call this concept overgeneralization, which is when we see something as all bad or all good. This limits our ability of seeing our whole selves, with good and bad. An extreme example of this is our opinion of murderers. All we can think of is their offense. Although their crime is deplorable, the truth is that their crime is not all that defines their character. It's quite possible that they have some positive parts. Those who know these offenders may describe some positive traits about them. I use this example not to offend anyone but to see in a very extreme case that there can be good and bad in all of us. What if we were to have our sins discussed in a court of law? We would be incredibly embarrassed and exposed in front of others. Those in the courtroom might look down on us and judge us for our filthy sins. In a real sense, we can see clearly our own negative characteristics. On the other hand, we also have glowingly positive traits that define who we are as well. Which do you relate more to: the positive or the negative parts? Which do you focus more on: the faults or strengths?

Do you have a motto for your life? How about the motto "I am better today than I was yesterday and will continue to strive and plunge forward"? Can we accept that it takes time to improve our lives and that there is nothing wrong with incremental progress? This mindset would likely take the pressure off of us to be super performers, superrich, super popular, or the best in our fields! Prioritizing industry over ambition would help us to accept our stations in life. We need to just keep focusing on working on our weaknesses with a grace to ourselves. Can we be gracious to ourselves in the same way that God shows us grace? The definition of *grace* is "unmerited favor." In a spiritual sense, we see God's grace as His goodness toward those who have no claim on or reason to expect divine favor. We find the dichotomy of there being good and bad in people. We should be content with our lives but also continue striving for purity and closeness with God.

On the topic of being content in our lives, there are a few scriptures that stand out. Philemon 4:11–12 tells us, "I am not saying this because I am in need, for *I have learned to be content whatever the circumstances. I have learned the secret of being content in any and every situation*" (italics mine). The other scripture is found in 1 Timothy 6:6. "But *godliness with contentment is great gain*" (italics mine). God wants us to be okay with where we are in life and to be content with that place. On the other hand, God also makes it clear that He wants us not to just stay in the place where we are but to continue to better ourselves. In Philemon 3:13–14, it says, "But one thing I do: Forgetting is behind and straining toward what is ahead.

I press on toward the goal to win the prize for which God has called me heavenward in Christ Jesus" (italics mine). Second Peter 1:5–8 also tells us this other side of striving ahead. "For this very reason, *make every effort to add to your faith, goodness;* and to goodness, *knowledge;* and to knowledge, *self-control;* and to self-control, *perseverance;* and to perseverance, *godliness;* and to godliness, *brotherly kindness;* and to brotherly kindness, *love.* For if you possess these qualities in increasing measure, they will keep you from being ineffective and unproductive in your knowledge of our Lord Jesus Christ" (italics mine).

We can be content with where we are in the process and put the failures and negative characteristics in the past. This allows us to plunge forward and make progress as well. We are all works in progress. We are all imperfect in many ways. But if we focus on Jesus and His example, we can continue to grow and change, overcome the negative characteristics, and make progress forward to become different. As Colossians 1:29 states, "To this end I *labor, struggling with all His energy, which so powerfully works in me*" (italics mine).

Part of developing a healthy self-esteem is making a commitment to not try to please the world only. Someone once said, "The one magic key to personal fulfillment may be forever illusive, but the sure key to failure is to try to please everyone." Rather than trying to chase the unattainable reward of pleasing everyone and changing God's truth by doing so, you can learn to stand up for what you believe, speak the truth in love, live through stormy times with energy and joy, and little by little rewrite your life script.

Listen to Mandisa's song "Unfinished."
Listen to Francesca Battistelli's "Giants Fall."
Listen to Hillsong's "Who You Say I Am."

What are your most glaringly obvious strengths and weaknesses? Write them down.

Do you find it difficult to find contentment in your life?

Do you let others' opinions of you define your self-worth?

Do you know how to be gracious to yourself and your faults?

Who gives us the strength to overcome and strive ahead?

TWENTY-FOUR

BE HEALTHY

You may be wondering what being healthy has to do with the concept of self-esteem. Well, there are many ways that taking care of your body, which is the temple where God lives, can help you have positive feelings about yourself. You've probably heard of the concept that if you put trash in, you get trash out. If you do not take care of your own body, what you'll get is trash or negative feelings toward yourself and life. More specifically, I am talking about sleeping, eating, exercising, and keeping a balance in your life. This includes pleasurable activities, such as hobbies, traveling, and spending time with friends. You might be thinking that these specifics are basic, but I will explain specifically why they are very important to feeling good and being your best.

Sleep actually plays an important role in physical health. It helps heal and repair your heart and blood vessels. It is also important because it is linked to a number of brain functions. The nerve cells or neurons communicate with each other during sleep. Some research findings show that sleep plays a housekeeping role by removing from your brain toxins that build up in your system when you are awake. It also helps us to be more alert, supports learning and memory, and allows us to think more clearly. It reduces stress and boosts mood. Getting enough sleep, which is seven to nine hours a night, helps us be healthier. Not getting enough sleep can have serious health problems, such as heart disease, obesity, or diabetes. This also makes it more difficult for our bodies to handle stressors through the day and can contribute to increased impatience and anger. It is important to have a consistent bedtime. Also, destressing and journaling about the worries of the day before bedtime can be helpful. Getting enough sleep, especially quality sleep, is one key to a healthy lifestyle. When you wake feeling good and rested, you feel more positive about life and yourself.

What you feed your body is another important part of leading a healthy lifestyle. What you eat affects how your body feels. A well-balanced diet can provide the energy that you need to stay active through the day. The nutrients in your diet are needed for growth and repair and for helping you stay healthy and strong. So you are wondering, *What is a healthy eating regiment?* One that is rich in fruits, vegetables, whole grains, low-fat dairy, and protein. Drinking plenty of water helps your skin, energy, muscles, and kidneys. It helps you feel well and look good overall. Eating well can help to reduce the risk of heart disease by helping to maintain blood pressure and cholesterol levels as well as helping to prevent diabetes and some cancers. Having a good variety of the above foods every day leaves less room in your diet to eat foods high in fat and sugar. When you don't eat good food, it can contribute to stress, tiredness, illness, and health problems like obesity and tooth decay. Doctors have been able to see the signs of poor nutrition by patients displaying feelings of being tired, having brittle hair, dental problems, a change in bowel habits, mood and mental health issues, easily bruising, healing slowly, and a having a slow immune response. Having a well-balanced diet combined with regular exercise are cornerstones to good health. And we all know that when you eat well and feel better, it increases self-esteem.

Physical exercise can have immediate and long-term health benefits and improve your quality of life. The benefits of exercise are strengthening the heart, helping keep the arteries and veins clear, reducing blood sugar levels, controlling weight, strengthening bones, helping to prevent cancer, and regulating blood pressure. Most importantly, regular activity can improve your quality of life. Wow. That's a lot of benefits to moving your body! Exercise boosts your energy and releases happy endorphins into your brain. This means that you will be happier and have more energy.

How does keeping balance in your life help you? The definition of *balance* is "a condition in which different elements are equal or in the correct proportions." So keeping balance in life is not cramming in every activity possible. Examine your values and decide from there which activities should be added and which should be let go. Then set boundaries. Boundaries just mean that you have to say no to some activities. Be organized and plan what you would like to fill each week with ahead of time. There will be work, recreation, and quality time with family and friends. Don't take on too many projects at one time. When the unexpected happens, don't get stressed. Learn to be flexible when things happen that you have no control over. Be able to adjust your game plan.

First Corinthians 12:27 helps us to understand why we should take care of ourselves. "Now you are the body of Christ and each one of you is a part of it. We represent the body of Christ. How would we want that body to be represented? Do you not know that your *bodies are the temples of the Holy Spirit,* who is in you, whom you have received from God? You are not your own; you were bought at a price. Therefore honor God with your bodies" (1 Corinthians 6:19–20; italics mine).

Our bodies are not our own. Christ paid His own life for us. How then should we take care of our bodies? It states that we should honor God with our bodies. This means that we are to take care of ourselves and honor God with our bodies. We are to take care of ourselves so that we can be a great representation of His temple and to show our appreciation for His sacrifice. The scriptures tell us in 1 Corinthians 3:16–17 again that we are God's temple. "Don't you know that *you yourselves are God's temple and that God's Spirit dwells in your midst?* If anyone destroys God's temple, God will destroy that person; for *God's temple is sacred, and you together are that temple*" (italics mine). We need to treat our bodies as sacred. We should be aware that when we do not take care of ourselves by eating, sleeping, and exercising, we are destroying God's temple. Our bodies are the temples of God that we need to take care of.

To close out this chapter, I am going to leave you with a scripture from Romans 12:1. "Therefore, I urge you, brothers and sisters, in view of God's mercy, to *offer your bodies as a living sacrifice, holy and pleasing to God-this is your true and proper worship*" (italics mine).

Listen to Matthew West's song "The Motions."

What keeps you from taking care of your body?

Why does God want us to be our best?

Why should we take care of ourselves?

What is most difficult for you: eating, sleeping, exercising, or keeping balance?

TWENTY-FIVE

WRAP-UP

This book has been about trying to help us gain perspective on how we should look and feel about ourselves. The world has many ways that affect our self-esteem. Many of those things are contrary to what God feels about us. We have the gift of being able to gain the proper perspective of who we really are. We are not just who the world says that we are. We are who God says we are.

If all of us were good-looking, smart, popular, successful academically as well as occupationally, involved in impressive activities, in touch with our nationalities, loved our bodies, were rich, and had many social media followers, then we would fit the mold for every category in the world's definition of someone with high self-esteem. The reality is that most of us do not fit all these categories, so we are left wanting more and thinking less of ourselves. Most of the above categories often change at some time in our lives. Do the above categories really define success in life? You see, we were all created by our Maker, so we are technically who He created us to be. We can't trade ourselves in for newer models, nor should we redefine God's perfect plan. God does not create any junk. He created you entirely as He wanted you to be.

God tells us that we are lovable masterpieces whose God-given talents are important. He has plans for us, we are stable, we are in the royal family, all nations are equal, we have hope, we are given top-secret information, our mistakes are forgotten, and we are rich. If we understand that wonderful, awesome view that God has of us and accept it both mentally and emotionally, then we can have the self-esteem that God created us to have. We can marvel in His amazing plan that He established for our lives at the creation of the world.

Above anything else, He wants us to understand how much He loves us and how important we are in His eyes. He wants us to be dearly loved and cherished in so many ways. Colossians 3:1–2 tells us that very thing. "Since, then, you have been *raised with Christ, set your hearts on things above*, where Christ is, seated at the right hand of God. *Set your minds on things above, not on earthly things*" (italics mine). This scripture helps us to acknowledge that we need to engage our hearts and our minds not in the things of the world but in the things above. We should and need to be focused on God's heart and thoughts. This is how we truly become confident and gain a strong self-esteem.

Look at life from God's perspective and seek after what He desires. Get into your Bible daily and ask Him to reveal His view of you. Ask Him to help you to let go of the world defining you. Seek to hear His voice, and thank Him for the work that He's doing in your life. Proverbs 3:5–6 tells us, "*Trust in the Lord with all your heart and lean not on your own understanding*; in *all of your ways submit* to Him, and He will *make your paths straight*" (italics mine). God delights in us, and He promises to help us to thrive and to continue to grow and become firmly planted. Psalm 37:23–24 tells us, "If the *Lord delights in a man's way*, He *makes His steps firm*; though he stumbles, he will not fall, for the *Lord upholds him with His hand*" (italics mine). God is the one who helps us live lives representative of Him. As we learn to accept who we are in God's sight, He helps us to take steps, even if they are baby steps, and keeps us firm.

We also need to delight in God. "*Delight yourself in the Lord* and He will *give you the desires of your heart*" (Psalm 37:4; italics mine). Our desire is to be special, loved, important, and relevant, and to make a difference. God tells us that if we see what's important about ourselves, we will begin to see His amazing plan for our lives. If only we could see clearly through God's eyes His view of us, we would be able to capture our true worth. Hurtful experiences can erode our confidence in who we really are. There is a tendency to link our identities to our past failures. Regardless of our failures, whether big or small, we must not identify ourselves by the sins in the past that we have been forgiven for and for which have asked others for forgiveness. Some of us identify ourselves by our past sins. God forgives us for those sins and calls us sons and daughters. We are in His royal family. I have found great comfort and strength in knowing that I am a child of God—unconditionally, without question, and forever in my heavenly Father's family. A biblical example of this is that even though David committed adultery, he was called a man after God's own heart. Even though Abraham lied three times, he was known as the Father of the Faithful. Paul persecuted the Christians and helped put them to death, yet he penned much of the New Testament and helped spread the gospel. What is true about all these biblical examples is that the men took responsibility for their sins and pursued God wholeheartedly.

Spiritual markers of a healthy self-esteem are first and foremost keeping a humble attitude. Second, speak truth in love to others, without the fear of being judged. Third, learn to separate your feelings from a message being delivered. There may be helpful parts of the message. Fourth, learn to understand your emotions and the emotions of others. Learn to look at the message under the emotions of others. Fifth, be accountable in word and deed, and let them be one and the same. Increasing your self-esteem is accomplished by taking baby steps and truly finding the will that our Father has for our lives.

Go back to part 1 and identify the misperceptions in the areas that are holding you back from understanding completely, both mentally and emotionally, the perception that God wants you to fully understand, and let it envelop you. Let it wrap around you so that you can feel and experience how God truly feels about you.

ABOUT THE AUTHOR

Kathy Sebo, a licensed clinical social worker, has helped many families, children, and adults over her thirty-year career. She has presented a variety of workshops around the Midwest. She currently works in a private practice and has based her book on years of observing wrong thinking. She hopes that through God's scriptures, she can help others change their thoughts of their worth.

Printed in the United States
By Bookmasters